KAYAK FISHING
The Ultimate Guide

2nd Edition

By Scott Null and Joel McBride

THE **HELICONIA PRESS**

PUBLISHED BY

 THE **HELICONIA PRESS**

1576 Beachburg Road
Beachburg, Ontario
K0J 1C0 Canada
www.helipress.com

Written by:	SCOTT NULL AND JOEL McBRIDE
Edited by:	TIM SHUFF
Photography by:	JOCK BRADLEY, except as noted
Illustrations by:	PAUL MASON
Design and Layout by:	BETH KENNEDY

Library and Archives Canada Cataloguing in Publication.

Null, Scott, 1963-
Kayak fishing : the ultimate guide / by Scott Null and
Joel McBride. -- 2nd ed.

ISBN 978-1-896980-43-0

1. Kayaking. 2. Fishing--Handbooks, manuals, etc.
I. McBride, Joel, 1966- II. Title.

SH446.K39N84 2009 799.12 C2008-907345-2

ABOUT SAFETY
Kayak fishing is an activity with inherent
risks, and this book is designed as
a general guide, not a substitute for
experience. The publisher and the
authors do not take responsibility for the
use of any of the materials or methods
described in this book. By following any
of the procedures described within, you
do so at your own risk.

Contents

About the Authors	**7**
Photography	**8**
Special Contributors	**9**
Foreword	**17**

Chapter 1: Equipment	**19**
Kayaks	**20**
Sit-On-Top Kayaks (SOTs)	21
Sit-Insides (SINKs)	23
Choosing a Kayak	24
What Are Kayaks Made From?	24
A Quick History of the Kayak	27
Paddles	28
PFDs (Personal Flotation Device)	31
Dressing for Kayaking	**33**
Dressing for Warm Water Conditions	33
Dressing for Cold Water Conditions	33
Safety Gear	**36**
Water and Energy Bars	37
First Aid Kit	37
Emergency Bag	37
Spare Paddle	37
Paddle Floats	37
Bilge Pumps	37
Communication Devices	38
Cell Phones	38
VHF Radios	38
Signaling Devices	39
Whistles	39
Strobes	39
Flares And Smoke	39
Reflectors	39

Navigation Tools	39
Charts	40
Compasses	40
Tide and Current Tables	40
Gps Units	40

Chapter 2: Outfitting your Kayak	**41**
Accessories	**43**
Seats	43
Rod Holders	43
Paddle Holders	46
Paddle Leashes	47
Anchors	47
Stake-Out Pole	48
Live Bait Tanks	51
Fish Finders and Depth Sounders	52
Thigh Straps	53
Rudders	54
Pontoons / Outriggers	54
Packing Your Kayak	**55**
Dry Stowage	55
Installing Accessories	**56**
Fastening Options	56
Installing a Flush Mount Rod Holder or Receiver	57
Installing Fish Finders	58
Mounting the Transducer	58
Mounting Display Unit	59
Batteries	60
Mounting The Battery Box	60
Installing Paddle Clips	61
Outfitting with the Pros	**62**
"Bluewater Jon Schwartz	62

Mark Pierpont	63
Dean "Slowride" Thomas	64
Jimbo Meador	65
Chad Hoover	66
"Kayak Kevin" Whitley	67
Jeffrey Goudreau	68
Howard McKim	69
Chris LeMessurier	70

Chapter 3: Before Hitting the Water	**71**
Care and Maintenance for Your Kayak and Gear	**73**
Transporting Your Kayak	73
Carrying Your Kayak	75
Getting In and Out of Your Kayak	77
Using Your Paddle	78
Choosing a Kayak Fishing Location	81

Chapter 4: The Essential Strokes and Paddling Techniques	**83**
Forward Stroke	**84**
Catch	86
Rotation	86
Recovery	86
Reverse Stroke	**88**
Using the Reverse Stroke as a Brake	89
Sweep Strokes	**90**
Forward Sweep	90
Reverse Sweep	92
Draw Strokes	**94**

Contents

Basic Draw   94
T-Stroke Draw   95
Sculling Draw   96

Your Kayak in Motion   98
Weathercocking   100

Paddling in Windy Conditions   101
Using Rudders or Skegs   102

Re-entering Your Kayak from the Water 104
Re-entering a Sit-On-Top   104
Re-entering a Sit-Inside   106

**Chapter 5:
Fishing from a Kayak   109**

Fighting Fish from a Kayak   112

Landing Fish in a Kayak   117

Big Game Kayak Fishing   121
Big-Game Gear   124
Fighting Big Fish   125
The End Game   127

Kayak Fishing Techniques   129
Trolling   130
Drift Fishing   132
Side-Saddle Fishing   133
Poling   134
Wade Fishing from the Kayak   136
Kayak Fly Fishing   136
Using Bait   139
Using Lures   140
Using Anchors   140
Fishing from a Tandem   141
Fishing with Kids   142
Using a Power Boat as a Mothership   143

**Chapter 6:
Freshwater Kayak Fishing   145**

Kayak Fishing the Great Lakes   146
Places to Kayak Fish   146
Fish Targeted   148
Safety   148

Kayak Fishing for Bass   149
Gearing up   151
Think Like a Fish   152
Bait Versus Lures   152

Kayak Fishing for Muskie   153
Finding Muskies   153
Tackle for Muskies   154
Live Bait   155
Presentation Strategies   155
Landing Muskies in a Kayak   156

Fishing Flowing Rivers   157
Classes of Rivers   157
Basic Current Dynamics   159
Getting to the Fish—Paddling in Current   160
    Eddy Turns   161
    Ferrying   162
    Handling Rocks   162
    Swimming In Current   164
River Hazards and Safety   165
    Strainers   165
    Low Head Dams   166
    Foot Entrapment   166
    Using Anchors   167

**Chapter 7:
Saltwater Kayak Fishing   169**

Understanding Tides and Tidal Currents 170

Dealing with Surf   173
Choosing a Beach   173
Kayaks for Surf Zones   174
Launching in Surf   175
Landing in Surf   178

Saltwater Fishing Hazards and Safety   180
Sharks   181
Stingrays   181
Other Creatures   182
Weather   182
Tides and Currents   183
The Other Guy   184

Kayak Fishing Florida   185
East Coast   186

The Keys and Florida Bay   188
Gulf Coast   189
Panhandle   192

Kayak Fishing Texas   193
Coastal Inshore Waters   194
Lakes and Ponds   194
Rivers and Streams   194
The Surf Zone and Offshore Waters   195
Resources   195

**California Dreamin': Exploring the Golden
State's Spectacular Kayak Fishing   197**
Southern California's Bountiful Ocean   198
The Rugged North   199
Getting Fresh   200
California's Slick Sleds   200
A Lifetime's Worth of Kayak Fishing Water   200

Kayak Fishing East Coast Style   201
Northeast   202
Georgia   203
North Carolina   204
Virginia   205

Kayak Fishing Alaska Style   207

**Chapter 8:
Kayak Fishing Safety   211**

Dealing with Weather   213

Choosing a Safe Fishing Location   214

Kayak Fishing Alone   215

Kayak Fishing in Exposed Conditions   216
Exposed Water Equipment Considerations   216
    Seaworthy Kayaks   216
    Safety Gear and Accessories   217
Communicating   218
    Whistle   218
    Paddle   218
    Boat Support   218
Navigating   218
Towing   219

Glossary of Terms   220

About the Authors

Captain Scott Null

Captain Scott Null grew up fishing the waters of the Galveston Bay Complex and has hunted and fished on the Texas coast his whole life. Spurred by his adventurous spirit and desire to explore new waters, he has fished all along the Gulf Coast, from the southern tip of Texas to the Florida Everglades.

Scott spends most of his time in the marshes, bayous, and flats of the Upper Texas Coast, where he uses a kayak to stalk shallow foraging redfish. When he isn't fishing for himself he shares his love of the outdoors and extensive knowledge with others through his guiding company Let's Go Fishing.

Scott is a retired homicide detective who worked for the Houston Police Department for 21 years. Scott is now a regional sales representative for Mid-South Sports selling a wide variety of fishing, hunting, and camping equipment to outdoors shops throughout southeast Texas, Louisiana and Mississippi. He also writes a monthly column on kayak fishing for *Texas Saltwater Fishing Magazine* and has authored several fishing articles for Paddler Magazine.

Joel McBride

Joel McBride is a passionate and knowledgeable whitewater kayaker and fisherman, having frequently paddled and fished both rivers and freshwater lakes since he was a boy growing up in Maine. Joel lives along the banks of the Arkansas River with his wife and two daughters in the small, mountain town of Salida, Colorado. He has worked in sales and marketing for the most prominent paddlesports manufacturers for the past 15 years and although his days are busy, he never misses an opportunity to get his feet wet.

Photography

Jock Bradley

Whether bushwhacking through Philippine jungles, rappelling into vertical gorges or diving into ocean depths, Jock consistently overcomes tremendous obstacles to obtain the perfect shot. It is, above all, this type of dedication and work ethic that sets him apart—making him one of the world's foremost professional outdoor photographers. For more info, visit www.jockbradley.com.

Special Contributors

Greg Bowdish

Originally from Georgia, Greg Bowdish moved to Florida for the great shallow-water fishing over a decade ago. He spent several years building fishing boats before becoming an FFF certified fly casting instructor, a popular speaker at fishing clubs and shows and a regular outdoor writer and photographer for numerous fishing publications. Greg is also a member of the Ocean Kayak Pro Staff and an active advisor toward the design and development of new kayaks. For more information about Greg's activities or about his fly fishing and kayak fishing guided trips, visit www.kayak-fish-florida.com.

Mark Ezell

Mark began kayak fishing in 1997 and has fished the central and southern coast of California and both sides of Baja, Mexico. It was right in his backyard near Dana Point, California, that he caught his largest halibut to date, a 20-pounder, on 8-pound-test. When fellow fishermen started asking him where he got some of the products on his kayak, he and his wife Karen started their online store, Hook 1 Kayak Fishing Gear. They've been selling online since 2002 and supporting the kayak fishing community by giving donations at tournaments ever since. Hook 1's website is chock-full of useful information, how-tos, and pictures of rigged kayaks that benefit every level of kayak fisherman and woman, at www. kayakfishinggear.com.

Chad Hoover

Chad grew up hunting and fishing in rural Louisiana and Georgia and is now an active-duty naval officer stationed in Norfolk, Virginia. He developed a passion for saltwater flats kayak fishing while assigned to a search and Rescue unit in Corpus Christi, Texas. He has since pursued nearly every available species along the Gulf of Mexico and the East Coast; however, trophy largemouth bass are his true passion. Chad is an accomplished tournament angler and conducts seminars and clinics throughout the Mid-Atlantic and Southeast. He is a member of the Wilderness Systems Kayak Fishing Team and author of the new book *Kayak Fishing for Bass*, from The Heliconia Press.

Everett (EJ) and Pam Johnson

EJ and Pam are probably two of the busiest people in the Texas outdoors scene. Together, they run Gulf Coast Connections Guide Service, guiding anglers by powerboat and kayak to some of the most pristine marshes on the Texas Coast, located along the back side of Matagorda Island. Not only can EJ guide you to some awesome fishing, he can also provide you with a running narrative on the history and natural wonders of the area. On top of all this, EJ and Pam publish *Texas Saltwater Fishing Magazine,* the only publication dedicated solely to the Texas saltwater fishing enthusiast. For guided trips, contact EJ or Pam at 361-550-3637. For more information about the magazine, go to www.texassaltwater-fishingmagazine.com.

Paul Lebowitz

Paul hasn't looked back since he first hopped on a kayak to catch a yellowtail in his home state of California. Now one of kayak fishing's most widely published writers, Paul has an award-winning monthly column at the nation's largest outdoor weekly, *Western Outdoor News,* and is a regular contributor to *Canoe and Kayak* and *Kayak Angler* magazines. Paul is the founding director of the Kayak Fishing Association of California, a grassroots organization dedicated to "preserve and expand kayak fishing opportunities." Many of his stories are free for the reading at his website www. KayakFishingZone.com.

Chris LeMessurier

Born and raised in Michigan, Chris has been obsessed with fishing from a young age and has spent many days chasing fish on the Great Lakes. He started kayak fishing in 2005 with what he thought was an epiphany, combining fishing and kayaking, until he did a quick Google search and realized that many had come before him. He targets everything from the tasty salmon to the explosive northern pike and muskie. Chris is a member of the Hook 1 Crew, the Wilderness Systems Kayak Pro Fishing Team and the Michigan Kayak Fishing Team, which can be found online at www. MichiganKayakFishing.com.

Brendan Mark

Growing up on the Ottawa River, Brendan has been both a dedicated paddler and an angler since he was kid. Throughout his teens and early twenties, Brendan committed himself to his obsession with whitewater kayaking and reached his ultimate paddling goal in 2003 by winning the World Championships in Austria. Shortly thereafter, having retired from competitive kayaking, Brendan realized that he could combine his two favorite activities—whitewater kayaking and fishing—and discovered that it allowed him to access huge stretches of water that have likely never seen lures. With an honors business degree in marketing and a passion for the outdoors, Brendan is the marketing director for The Heliconia Press—publishers of this book.

Howard McKim

Howard grew up in Texas, a long way from his current home of Ketchikan, Alaska. After finishing an anthropology major in college, he moved to San Diego and quickly fell in love with the ocean, scuba diving, and jetty and surf fishing. The desire to get further out led to his first kayak, and that first kayak led to a whole new life. Not long afterwards, Howard made the big move up to Alaska, where he started his guiding business, Ketchikan Kayak Fishing, and became Southeast Alaska's number-one kayak fishing guide. For more information on Howard's trips, visit www.yakfishalaska.com.

Jamie Pistilli

Jamie has been fishing the waters of North America and the Caribbean for over 20 years, and although he has caught everything from tarpon to sharks, his specialty is trophy muskie and carp. Jamie has been featured in numerous fishing publications and is a regional editor for *Kayak Angler* magazine. He's also a member of the Ocean Kayak Pro Staff and an active advisor, guide and fishing consultant in Ottawa, Ontario. For more information about Jamie's activities and guiding services, visit www. thefishingconsultant.com.

Jim Sammons

A San Diego California native and certified fish and game licensed guide, Jim has spent most of his life on or near the water. In 1995 he started La Jolla Kayak Fishing guide service and has been at the leading edge ever since. Recognized world wide as a pioneer of big game kayak fishing, Jim has probably caught more big fish from a kayak than anyone. As one of the original Ocean Kayak Pro Anglers, Jim has been closely involved with the development of new boat designs. Jim also works with Shimano on their kayak fishing line. To find out more about Jim's activities and the La Jolla Kayak Fishing trips in both San Diego and Baja, visit www.kayak4fish.com.

Dean "Slowride" Thomas

Dean and his wife Jennifer run Slowride Guide Service in Aransas Pass, Texas. Dean plies his trade in the Redfish Bay area which is one of the most popular kayak fishing destinations on the Texas coast. These shallow grass flats are home to a healthy population of speckled trout and redfish, and Dean knows the flats better than anyone. Whether you are looking for a fully guided fishing trip or just want to rent a kayak and go exploring on your own, the Thomas duo will take great care of you. Check out their website, www.slowrideguide.com.

Kevin Whitley

Ever since kayak fishing entered the Mid-Atlantic fishing scene, "Kayak Kevin" has blazed the trail to what is possible while fishing from a kayak. Kayak Kevin is the first kayak angler to be recognized by the Virginia Saltwater Fishing Tournament as an Expert Saltwater Angler, a status awarded to those who land six different, trophy-sized species in a year. Kevin has reached this prestigious level two years in a row. Kevin has also completed five long-distance, solo kayak tours in the last six years, with the longest being 1,800 miles from Pensacola, Florida, to his home in Norfolk, Virginia. His website is www.kayakkevin.com.

Ken Whiting

The Heliconia Press is led by World Champion whitewater kayaker Ken Whiting. Ken is one of the most influential and respected paddlers in the world, and was recognized as such by *Paddler* magazine as one of their "Paddlers of the Century." After discovering kayak fishing in 2006, Ken's life was forever changed. His new-found obsession for the sport led to the publishing of this book. These days, you'll either find Ken on the river kayak fishing, or in the office planning the next kayak fishing adventure.

Charles (Chuck) Wright

Captain Wright owns and operates Chokoloskee Charters in the heart of the Everglades. From his home on the water, he guides fishermen to the remote reaches of the last great frontier of fishing in the continental United States. When you climb aboard his 28-foot mothership *Yak Attack*, you're beginning the adventure of a lifetime. Captain Chuck uses the boat to transport people and kayaks to areas of the Everglades that seldom see an angler, much less a kayak angler. Paddling deep into the Everglades is a truly special experience, and Chuck is the right guy to make it happen. To get in touch with Captain Wright go to www.chokoloskeecharters.com.

Introduction

BY SCOTT NULL

FISHING FROM A KAYAK? Sounds crazy to those who have never heard of it or experienced it, but kayak fishing is currently one of the fastest growing sports in America. Even the most ardent wade anglers and skiff anglers are easily lured into kayak fishing by its ease of use and the access it provides to new waters.

I often get the question, "Why would you fish from a kayak when you've got a perfectly good boat?" I have a standard answer for this near-constant question: I use a kayak so that I can go where it's too shallow for boats and too muddy for wading. My home waters are the Galveston Bay Complex. You'd be hard pressed to find an area on the Texas coast with more fishing pressure than this bay system. The kayak has allowed me to explore and fish in places that are virtually inaccessible to powerboat—and in the process I've managed to escape the crowds and find fish that rarely see a lure.

Even though this was the main reason I got into fishing from a kayak, I've come to learn that kayaks are great for all kinds of fishing. I can paddle out to the open bay and drift a reef or I can bust through the surf and fish the outer bar in relative comfort. They're also perfectly at home on a small stream or a big freshwater lake. I've even paddled several miles out into the Gulf of Mexico seeking bigger and meaner game fish. Modern kayaks are one of the most versatile and easy-to-use crafts available. There are all kinds of kayaks designed to fit a wide variety of people and fishing situations. Just match the kayak to the job and head out on your adventure.

A kayak fishing trip can be as simple or as complex as you want. A quick trip to a nearby waterway after work can be a perfect end to a stressful day. I've found that these trips can happen frequently because they don't take much pre-trip planning; nor do they require much in the way of post-trip chores. I keep my basic kayak fishing gear stowed in the garage, where it is easy to grab on a moment's notice. I drive to the shore, put the kayak in the water, and go. It's truly amazing what a couple hours on the water can do for the psyche. When the trip is over, if I don't have time to clean the boat, it can wait until tomorrow or even the next day. I can even skip the late evening chore of unloading the kayak from the truck by simply locking it in place. There is some smug satisfaction to be had while driving through traffic the next morning with a kayak still strapped to the truck.

Contrast this scenario with a trip in my pre-kayak days. Does the boat have gas? How's the battery? Are the wheel bearings greased? Then it was time to hook up the boat and tow it to a ramp, pay the ramp fee, launch the boat, and park the truck before I even got around to thinking about any fishing. When the trip was over, it was time to clean up the boat, flush the engine with fresh water, and drop it off at the storage shed. Over the years, I had come to the point where quick trips after work just weren't worth the effort. A busy day at work followed by a hectic scramble to get in a couple hours of fishing was not exactly relaxing and therapeutic.

This book was born as an idea for prompting people with fishing skills who were on the fence about kayak fishing to go ahead and jump in. As the project progressed, we realized that many longtime kayakers were likely thinking about getting into it from the other direction, so we added some content for them. Now that it's done, I'm confident that this book offers new kayak anglers a solid foundation in skills and concepts that will allow a safe, comfortable entry into the sport. At the same time, experienced kayak anglers will learn how to get the most out of their time spent on the water. Ultimately, whether you're new to kayak fishing or already experienced, it is our hope that this book serves to make your experiences on the water safer, more productive, and most of all, more enjoyable.

Foreword

IT IS MY PRIVILEGE to write the foreword to Scott Null and Joel McBride's book, *Kayak Fishing: The Ultimate Guide*. I know them both very well and can vouch for their character, their knowledge, their enthusiasm and their desire to help others experience and enjoy the unique world of kayak fishing. Scott has been a lifelong coastal fisherman with nearly 30 years of experience here in Texas. The considerable knowledge he has gained as a recreational angler, tourney angler, charter captain and kayak fishing guide makes him a perfect candidate to author a book like this. Joel grew up in Maine and has made his home in Colorado for the past 20 years. Joel has a great passion for whitewater paddling, and mountain stream and river angling. He also brings a wealth of valuable experience to the authoring of this book. Scott and Joel have been very influential in guiding the sport of kayak fishing during its infancy, and continue to do so now, when it is enjoying immense popularity in many parts of this country.

It wasn't very long ago that if you carried a kayak on your vehicle, or paddled onto the flats or into the salt marshes of Texas, pretty near everybody who saw you would scratch their heads and ask whether you'd lost your marbles. Texas, you see, was the birthplace—and is still a stronghold—of shallow water skiffs that can traverse the flats and that seem able to glide on little more than dew. Serious shallow-water enthusiasts can be likened to cowboys in a way; neither could be considered fond of dismounting—especially if their next mode of transport required a paddle!

My personal paddlesport experiences span more decades than I like to admit, and so kayak fishing, when I got the chance, seemed a natural thing for me. It was introduced to me in the earlier days by several old salts who "mother-shipped" their plastic boats to the backcountry in vessels that drafted in feet, not the mere inches that redfish are very happy to thrive in. The game then was simple; when the fish were in the marsh, you'd run the big boat as close as you could, and then paddle in after them. The boats that were available to early kayak fishermen were hardly designed for the purpose, so we tried not to paddle any farther than necessary, and the stuff we equipped our boats with was almost comical—unless you were the guy trying to use it. In fact, many of us struggled through an assortment of pirogues, canoes, inflatables and various touring boats that we tried to adapt as fishing crafts before finally acquiring a modern, sit-on-top boat that was designed entirely for fishing.

We can thank Scott and Joel and others like them for their contributions to modern day design. The boats we have today are a joy to paddle and are designed to accept a dizzying array of accessories and accoutrements that make our fishing more fun and productive. When I think of some of the junk I've paddled and some of the crazy ideas my fishing buddies and I have tried, I am quick to say, "Read this book carefully and pay attention to what Scott and Joel have to say. You can become an expert kayak fisherman in a short time." The knowledge that you can acquire from reading this book will save you a lot of the grief the old-timers had to experience.

Today, we see kayak fishing really coming into its own. We have more people paddling right from the dock to the fishing grounds than we had back when mothershipping was considered the hot setup. Scott and Joel have put this book together in such a way that I believe there is important knowledge here for paddlers and anglers of all skill levels. The advice they give for rigging and equipping your boat and selecting your gear will be invaluable to beginners; and, no matter how many times you've done it on your own, ideas, observations, and recommendations from true experts are always worth your time and consideration. I hope that you will find this book as entertaining and informative as I have.

Wishing you all the best in fishing and paddling,

EVERETT JOHNSON
Editor and Publisher
Texas Saltwater Fishing Magazine

equipment

KAYAKS · PADDLES · PFDS · DRESSING FOR KAYAKING · SAFETY GEAR

Kayaks

WITH THE SPORT of kayak fishing growing at a steady rate, there are more than a few manufacturers producing kayaks intended specifically for kayak fishing. If you're just getting into the sport, the number of different boat designs available can make choosing a kayak seem overwhelming. It doesn't have to be. By clearly identifying how and where you'll be using the kayak, you can quickly narrow down your options. In particular, it will let you decide which of the two self-explanatory styles you should be considering; a Sit-On-Top kayak (SOT) or a Sit-Inside kayak (SINK).

Both SOTs and SINKs are available as hard shell boats and as inflatables. Hard shells are generally more popular because they require no set up. Inflatable kayaks are an option that some might consider because they are much easier to transport when they've been deflated. However, there are some points to consider before choosing an inflatable. Keep in mind the type of terrain you'll be fishing. Are there sharp rocks, downed trees, or shallow oysters? How about the hooks you're using and sharp teeth of some fish? Unless it is your only option, we would suggest you steer away from inflatable kayaks for serious fishing because of the ever-present danger of a puncture that could compromise your safety.

Although SOTs and SINKs have some differences, they share many of the same parts. The top of a kayak is referred to as the deck. The bottom is the hull. The front of the boat is called the bow, the back is the stern, and most will have carrying handles at each end. Some kayaks also have rudders or skegs to assist you in tracking (going straight) or steering. SOTs and SINKs both have seats and some form of support for the feet. The better models tend to have built-in backrests, although some of the best backrests are bought separately from the kayak and are then installed.

The differences between SOTs and SINKs are quite simple. With an SOT, your seating area is literally on the top deck of the kayak. With a SINK, you are sitting inside the craft, in a cockpit. Around the cockpit of a SINK you'll find the cockpit rim, otherwise referred to as the coaming. This raised lip allows a skirt to be attached to the boat in order to keep water out or sun off the legs. SINKs have foot pedals which can be adjusted inside, fore and aft, to accommodate paddlers with different leg lengths. While many SOT kayaks also have foot pedals, some only have foot wells. Foot wells are a series of bumps that protrude from the kayak at measured intervals, in which you place your feet. Foot wells are nice and

Sit-on-top kayak

Sit-inside kayak

simple, but foot pedals provide the most support and are more comfortable to use, especially if you're spending a full day on the water. Foot pedals are also necessary to control the rudder if the kayak is equipped with one.

Now that we've looked at the main similarities and differences between SOTs and SINKs, let's look at their advantages and disadvantages.

Sit-On-Top Kayaks (SOTs)

The sit-on-top is by far the most popular style of kayak for paddling anglers today, and for good reason. The SOT leaves you free to move about, sit side-saddle, or step off to wade fish with ease. The SOT also alleviates the fear that some people have of flipping upside-down and getting trapped inside their boat. If for some reason you did capsize (which is surprisingly hard to do), you'd simply fall off the kayak.

Most contemporary SOTs are designed with a hatch for stowage in the bow. This gives you ample room to bring extra clothing, lunch, and spare rods and reels. Just aft of the cockpit, you might find tank wells for easy access storage of spare tackle, a cooler, or your catch. Sit-on-tops are also "self-bailing,"

One of the many benefits of a sit-on-top kayak is that you can sit and cast from a side-saddle position.

meaning that water automatically drains out of the seat and off the deck through "scupper" holes that go right through the kayak. This means that unless your kayak suffers serious structural damage, you won't have to worry about swamping your boat.

There are a few downsides to SOTs that are worth considering. One is that they generally require more material than a SINK, so they tend to be a bit heavier. They are also usually wider than other kayaks, and although this makes them very stable, it also makes them less efficient to paddle. Another potential disadvantage is the fact that your lower body isn't protected, which means that you can expect your lower body to be wet when paddling an SOT, and exposed to the sun, wind and rain. This can be fine in warm environments, but if you're paddling in cold water, you'll need to wear clothing that will keep you warm even when it is wet.

Pedal Power

A few kayak manufacturers make pedal powered kayaks. The advantages of having your hands free to fish while your legs drive the boat are pretty obvious and very real. A disadvantage is that without a paddle you won't be nearly as maneuverable, which can make working a shoreline or dealing with current a bit more difficult. For those reasons, and for the sake of having a back-up plan in case of mechanical failure, you will likely want to bring a paddle anyway.

Sit-Insides (SINKs)

Sit-inside kayaks are more traditional and there are many to choose from. The best sit-inside kayaks for kayak fishing are found in the recreational category. Recreational sit-inside kayaks are recognizable by their big, open cockpits, which makes them extremely safe and minimizes any fears that one might have of being trapped inside. In fact, the cockpits are so large that you will easily fall out if you capsize. Even the most experienced kayakers couldn't keep themselves inside to perform an Eskimo roll if they were to flip. Most SINKs also come with hatches in the bow and stern, which are semi-waterproof because of walls inside the kayak called bulkheads. These bulkheads divide the boat's interior into separate compartments, which not only helps keep a relatively dry spot for your gear, but provides flotation for your kayak in the event your cockpit is swamped.

The advantage of SINKs is that they allow you to stay far drier and protect your lower body from the sun and wind. You can even use a spray skirt to help keep water and sun off your legs.

The downsides of using sit-inside kayaks for fishing are that you don't have the same freedom to move around on your kayak that you do with an SOT; nor can you just hop in and out of them while on the water. Sit-inside kayaks are not self-bailing; capsizing is also a much bigger issue because your boat will swamp.

The sit-inside kayak keeps you drier and protects your legs from sun and wind.

Choosing a Kayak

When trying to decide what type of kayak will best suit your needs, the most important questions you can ask yourself are how and where you'll be using your kayak. For example, if you live in the south and want to go fishing on the shallow coastal flats where the water is warm and the weather warmer, or if you plan to fish anywhere that it's nice to have the option of quickly hopping out of your kayak to wade fish, a sit-on-top will be the most practical choice. If you live in more northern or colder climates, or will be paddling in chillier water, a sit-inside might be the better boat for you.

Once you have decided on whether to go for a sit-on-top or sit-inside kayak, there are a few other issues to consider. As a general rule, the longer and narrower a boat is, the faster it will be. However, the wider a boat is, the more stable it will become, so narrower isn't necessarily better. Generally speaking, a short boat will be more maneuverable while a longer boat will track (go straight) more easily. Depending on where you'll spend your time and what waters you want to fish, this could be a very important point to consider. For open water situations and paddling longer distances, you might want to consider a longer kayak that is faster and tracks well. Should your

When deciding what type of kayak to buy, the most important question you need to answer is where you'll use it most of the time.

fishing adventures take you to small creeks or rivers, you would probably be better off with a shorter boat that will be easier to turn. Another factor to consider is that shorter boats are much easier to handle in transport and weigh considerably less than long ones. This can be an important consideration if you can foresee having to load your kayak by yourself.

WHAT ARE KAYAKS MADE FROM?

The vast majority of kayaks used for kayak fishing have hard shells made from roto-molded polyethylene—more commonly known as "plastic". Plastic kayaks are very affordable, incredibly durable, and they require virtually no maintenance. The only downside to plastic kayaks is their weight. Thermoformed boats are relatively new to the market and are

becoming somewhat more popular. The material used in the thermoforming process provides a great-looking kayak that is lighter, but it is not as resistant to impact as the roto molded boats. Inflatable kayaks are made from coated fabrics and the best ones are more durable than most paddlers would imagine, but durability and puncturing are still a concern.

| Spray Skirt |

The spray skirt, or spray deck, is responsible for covering the cockpit of a sit-inside kayak. For traditional kayaking, the skirt is designed to keep all water out of your boat, but for recreational kayaks (like kayak fishing boats), the skirt is usually made of a lighter material, and can be used to help keep water from splashing into your kayak and/or to help keep the sun off your legs. Skirts are definitely not an essential piece of gear for kayak fishing in sit-inside kayaks, but they can be helpful at times. You can even get a mini spray skirt, which only covers the cockpit in front of your body. This type of skirt is a much cooler option and offers the angler a nice platform for either stripping fly line or having lunch.

This Inuit seal hunter uses a traditional Greenland kayak made from seal sinew stretched over a wood frame. PHOTO BY VILLE MIETTINEN

A Quick History of the Kayak

The first kayaks were made thousands of years ago by the Inuit—the inhabitants of Greenland, northeastern Russia, Alaska and northern Canada, formerly known as Eskimos. Their kayaks were developed primarily as vehicles for hunting and fishing during the summer months, once the Arctic ice had broken. In fact, the word kayak literally means 'hunter's boat'.

These early kayaks were made by lashing bone and driftwood together with seal sinew or gut to create a frame. This frame was then wrapped in seal or caribou skin, sewn together, stretched taut and then dried. To waterproof the boats, boiled seal oil or caribou fat was smeared over the seams.

The original kayaks were made in a variety of shapes and sizes to accommodate the differing conditions in which they were being used. For example, a wider, larger kayak provided more storage space for game and supplies, and offered more stability in rough seas. On the other hand, longer and narrower kayaks were faster and allowed the paddler to cover more territory.

It wasn't really until 1907 that the kayak was discovered by the rest of the world, when a German inventor named Johann Klepper bought a design for a folding kayak from a student and began making kayaks with canvas stretched over a wooden frame. This marked the beginning of the kayak's use for recreational purposes.

Kayaking grew in popularity throughout Europe over the next 30 years and by the 1930s, folding kayaks were used for all types of paddling—including whitewater river running. In 1936, kayak racing became a part of the Olympic Games. During World War II, folding kayaks were even used for secret missions.

In the 1950s, the first fiberglass kayaks debuted. The stiffer construction material enhanced the craft's efficiency and durability. As the boats improved, the need for specialized skills such as the Eskimo roll slowed their mainstream appeal.

That changed in the 1970s with the advent of the self-draining sit-on-top kayak, particularly once new plastic rotomolding construction methods became common. Exemplified by Tim Nemier's Ocean Kayak Scupper, born on the beaches of Malibu, the open-deck design's forgiving, easy-on, easy-off nature and affordable pricing appealed to a broad outdoor audience. Unlike a canoe or traditional sit-inside kayak, they couldn't be swamped; through-deck scupper holes drain quickly.

The new style that was to evolve into the modern fishing kayak followed a time-honored tradition; it borrowed the best ideas from multiple sources. Inspired by the longboard—on calm days, some surfers paddle out to fish—and paired with the superior mobility of the kayak propelled by twin blades, its utility for divers and anglers was obvious.

Before long, demand for these stable, easy-to-use-boats soared, propelled by the emergence of the first kayak fishing guides and Internet pioneers such as Dennis Spike of KayakFishing.com. Both new and established paddlesports companies started producing kayaks designed specifically for fishing.

Fishing kayak evolution followed the normal path, that of fitting the boat to its environment. Thus, we have long, surf-capable open-water craft; short and nimble little river runners; and broad, flat-bottomed kayaks suited perfectly for sight-fishing skinny water. There are even pedal-powered models that dispense with the paddle—users of these "kick" boats have little reason to put down their fishing poles.

And so we've come full circle. The modern fishing kayak, mass-produced out of tough, inexpensive plastic, studded with rod holders and salted with fancy electronics, is ideally suited to its purpose. It looks nothing like the Inuit's original boat, painstakingly handmade of driftwood, skin and gut. At heart, they are the same. The hunter's spirit lives on.

This carbon fiber paddle with a bent shaft represents the high end in paddles. It is very light, strong, and stiff. The drip rings on the shaft prevent water from running down the blades and onto your hands.

Paddles

The paddle is one of the most important parts of the kayaking equation. It is the piece of equipment that translates your effort and energy into motion. Paddles come in a wide variety of shapes, sizes, and price ranges, so choosing one can be a daunting task for the beginner. If your kayak fishing excursions will keep you close to shore and close to where you started, almost any paddle will work. Just make sure that it is durable enough to stand up to the abuse that you will undoubtedly inflict upon it, and that it will effectively propel your kayak forward. However, if you will be traveling any real distance while kayak fishing, using a good quality paddle will make a big difference. The better paddles are lighter, stronger, and allow for more effective strokes, which will make your time on the water more comfortable and even more enjoyable. A lightweight, quality paddle also helps you avoid overuse injuries such as tendonitis in the wrist or elbow. As with most other sports these days, lighter equipment equals more money. Get the best paddle you can afford and you won't regret the extra dollars spent to shave those ounces.

Paddles have three main parts to them. They have a shaft, a power face, and a back face. The majority of the shafts you will see are straight, but you will likely run across several models with shafts that are bent. Bent shafts are intended to be more ergonomically correct and provide the paddler with a more comfortable grip. Some models accomplish this goal better than others. The power face is the side of the paddle blade that catches water when you take

Tip If your kayak fishing ever takes you far from shore, into water that is subject to strong winds or current, or anywhere else where losing or breaking a paddle would mean you've got a serious problem, bring a spare paddle along. As long as the spare can be broken down (into either two or four pieces) it can be easily stowed inside your kayak and out of the way.

A paddle with a 90-degree, 45-degree, and 0-degree feather.

a forward stroke. The back face is the side of the paddle that gets used for reverse strokes.

Kayak paddles are made from a variety of materials, although for casual paddling, plastic and fiberglass are by far the most common because they offer a great blend of performance, durability, and affordability. The lowest-priced paddles have an aluminum shaft and plastic blades. While these are adequate and will get the job done, they are often quite heavy and inefficient. The highest-end paddles are made with carbon fiber and are very light, strong, and stiff. These qualities make them the most efficient and pleasant paddles to use.

In general, paddles are measured in centimeters and range between 210 cm and 250 cm (roughly 6 ft to 8 ft). The proper length is chosen based on the paddler's height, arm length, and what feels most comfortable. Paddles between 220 cm and 235 cm are the most common and it's a fair bet that if you pick a paddle in this range you'll be happy with it. A paddle that is too short will not reach the water as well and your strokes will not get good

purchase. A paddle that is too long will feel cumbersome and will tire you out more quickly.

One thing to consider is that sit-on-top kayaks are usually a bit wider than their sit-inside brethren. You also sit higher on them, which means you have to reach a bit farther to the water. With this in mind, you may want to err on the longer side if you're paddling a sit-on-top. We like to use 225 cm paddles

Tip In shallow water, some kayak anglers like to bring along a pole so they can stand up and control the kayak, and get a better view. For more information about poling, see Chapter 4.

when paddling sit-inside kayaks, and 235 cm paddles for our sit-on-tops.

Paddles also come with a variety of blade shapes and sizes. For kayak fishing, large blades are nice to have. The larger blades assist in the propulsion of the less efficient SOT kayaks and they help you turn your boat more quickly while maneuvering to fight a fish.

A final decision that you'll need to make has to do with the feathering of the paddle. A "feathered" paddle has blades that are offset from one another. This lets the upper blade slice through the air and wind more easily while taking a forward stroke. The downside is that it requires the paddler to twist the paddle while moving from one stroke to the next. Some people find that this causes fatigue or pain in their wrists. A paddle with no feather is much more intuitive to use and is a good choice for most kayak anglers. Most paddles come as two-piece designs that offer the option of being assembled with or without feathered blades. Something to note is that these two-piece, adjustable paddles were designed to make paddles easier to transport, and to minimize the number of different paddles that stores needed to hold in inventory; not because you're supposed to adjust them all the time. Once you decide on and become comfortable using a paddle with a certain degree of offset, we wouldn't recommend changing it around.

PFDs (Personal Flotation Devices)

A PFD (lifejacket) is the single most important piece of equipment there is, and it should be worn whenever you're on the water. Of course, if it doesn't fit or isn't comfortable, you probably won't wear it. On a similar note, if a PFD is worn improperly, it can actually hinder, rather than help, your ability to swim. A good test for fit is to tighten the lifejacket as you would wear it, and then hook your thumbs under the shoulder straps and pull up. The jacket should stay in place on your torso and not lift in front of your face.

A kayak fishing-specific PFD keeps the flotation away from the shoulders and chest so that you're not restricted when paddling or casting. It also has convenient pockets for gear.

Any PFD that is Coast Guard approved, fits well, and is comfortable enough so you won't feel the need to remove it while on the water, is a perfectly adequate PFD. With that said, the best PFDs for kayak fishing are the ones that are designed specifically for the activity. There are now a number of kayak fishing PFDs to choose from. They all have a variety of pockets and keep the flotation away from the shoulders so they won't restrict your paddling or casting. Some have even removed the flotation from the lower back to accommodate the seats that many anglers use.

In warm climates, sun protection will be your main concern when deciding what to wear.

Dressing for Kayaking

Dressing for Warm Water Conditions

When the water is warm and the air temperature is even warmer, dressing properly for a day out on the water is easy. Your biggest concerns are staying protected from the sun's harmful rays and keeping hydrated. Of course, the best solution is to cover up and use sunscreen on any exposed skin. Even on the hottest day, a lightweight, long-sleeved shirt and long pants such as those made by Ex-Officio are a good idea because they keep the sun off the arms and body. There are some great quick-drying, ultra-light materials on the market that provide a good balance of sun protection and coolness. For those using a sit-inside kayak, a mini spray skirt is a good option. Because the mini-skirt only covers the front part of the cockpit, it keeps the sun off your lower extremities without turning your kayak into a sweatbox. On the feet, a good pair of water shoes or sandals like Tevas will always come in handy, although some areas warrant additional foot protection, especially if you plan to step off your kayak and wade fish.

Quality sunglasses are another important means of protecting yourself from the sun, particularly early or late

There's a reason why anglers like to use light, long-sleeved, quick drying shirts—they make life comfortable in the blistering heat.

in the day when the sun's glare off the water can be blinding. Get sunglasses that are polarized and provide good UV protection. The UV light rays are very harmful to your eyes. Of course, you'll want to have some type of retainer strap so that they can't fall into the water.

Dressing for Cold Water Conditions

When the air is warm and the water is cold, dressing appropriately can be a real challenge. No matter how warm the air is, swimming in cold water can drop your core body temperature to hypothermic levels at an alarming rate. On the flip side, being over-dressed in hot weather can result in heat stroke. The key is dressing in a way that keeps you cool enough when things are going well, yet warm enough in the event of a capsize. A neoprene wetsuit is one of the best options for these conditions. A neoprene Farmer John provides good insulation for a modest price, and the cut of the garment allows a full range of movement in the shoulder without chafing. A wetsuit is a great foundation piece for your paddling wardrobe because as temperatures drop, you can add more clothing for more warmth.

When both the water and the air temperature are cold, hypothermia becomes a serious hazard. You need to wear clothing that insulates well, both when dry and wet. This is where materials like fleece, polypropylene, and neoprene excel. Cotton is the worst option. Cotton dries very slowly and rather than insulating, it actually pulls heat away from your body. Wool is

Jim Sammons and Howard McKim both wear waterproof, breathable pants and jackets to stay warm in a chilly Alaskan environment.

another good option, although it gets really heavy when it's wet and takes forever to dry.

Over your insulating layers, you'll likely want to have an outer layer that keeps the wind off your body. Waterproof nylon jacket and pants work well. For your feet, try neoprene booties and a pair of wool socks. The ultimate outer-layer protection against the cold is a dry suit. A dry suit uses latex gaskets at the ankles, wrists and neck to keep all water out, even when you're completely immersed. Dry suits are expensive, but if you spend a lot of

time paddling in cold conditions it will be a great investment in terms of both comfort and safety.

Of course, the best strategy of all is to avoid capsizing altogether. By paddling in protected areas and fishing conservatively, capsizing is highly unlikely. Fishing kayaks are so stable that as long as you're paddling in a sheltered area that isn't subject to strong wind or waves, there's no reason to flip. As an added precaution, it's also important that you stay close to shore, so in the unlikely event that you capsize, you can quickly swim to

safety while your fishing buddies gather your equipment—when they're done laughing. The type of boat that you're paddling will also dictate how you'll need to dress in cold water. If you're paddling a sit-on-top kayak, you should prepare for your lower body to get wet, whereas a sit-inside will provide far more protection from the elements.

There are a number of other pieces of clothing that come in handy, and most kayaks have plenty of room to bring extra gear along. A wooly hat is a great addition on a chilly day, as are neoprene gloves, both of which will keep insulating

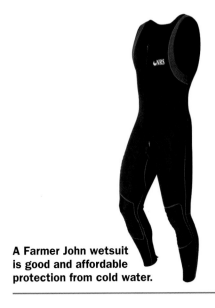

A Farmer John wetsuit is good and affordable protection from cold water.

if they get damp or wet. If you're using a sit-inside kayak, you can also wear a spray skirt to keep cold water out of your boat and allow your body heat to warm up the interior of the cockpit. Do yourself a favor and bring along a change of clothes stored in a dry bag. Should you unexpectedly become soaked on a cold day, you'll really appreciate this little nugget of advice.

Many people choose to wear waders to stay completely dry while kayaking. This is not a bad option, but it does require some forethought from a safety aspect. Waders full of water are very difficult to move around in and capsizing in deep water then becomes potentially deadly. To prevent large amounts of water getting inside your waders, you can wear a snug-fitting wading belt around the upper portion of the waders. This generally won't stop all of the water from entering, but it will slow the process down quite a bit, giving you more time to react and get yourself out of the bad situation.

Even a Southern Californian like Jim Sammons can be comfortable in the Alaska cold with the right gear. In this photo Jim wears a fleece hat, neoprene gloves, waders, and a paddling jacket over a few warm, insulating layers.

Most kayaks have lots of storage space, so there's no reason not to bring a dry bag with enough clothing to make sure you can stay warm no matter what.

Safety Gear

ALTHOUGH KAYAK FISHING is generally a very safe activity, as with anything, there is always the potential for things to go wrong. If things do go awry, having the equipment on hand to quickly and efficiently deal with the situation can make a huge difference. As a general rule, if there's even a chance that you could use something, then bring it along. Fishing kayaks have a lot of cargo space, so there's no reason not to, and as Murphy's Law states: If you don't bring it, you're going to need it.

The following is a list of basic safety equipment. Of course, every situation is different, so before each trip, you'll need to decide on what combination of safety gear makes the most sense. If you're just heading out on a small, protected lake for a quick after-work fish, you won't need much in the way of safety gear. Your best piece of safety equipment is your PFD, so make sure you're wearing it at all times. It's also a good idea to always bring a whistle.

On the other hand, if you plan on making a more adventurous trip, you might want to consider bringing a full complement of safety gear. These situations may include trips where you'll be paddling farther from shore than you can comfortably swim, venturing along rugged shorelines that don't provide easy escape from the water, or if the possibility exists that you will have to deal with waves, wind, or current. Remember too that safety equipment doesn't do any good if you don't know how to use it. So, if you want to fish in unsheltered, open water, especially with a sit-inside kayak (since you can't just hop back into it if you flip), you should consider getting professional instruction on kayak safety and rescue. For more information on safety issues relating to fishing in exposed water conditions, see Chapter 8, Kayak Fishing Safety.

Water and Energy Bars

It might not be something that you would consider safety gear, but since your body is the engine that drives your kayak forward, it's essential that it get enough fuel to do the job. Arguably more important than food is water. Staying hydrated will keep you warm and happily fishing all day long.

First Aid Kit

For obvious reasons, a first aid kit is always a good idea to bring along, and there are some great, ready-to-go kits available. Beyond the basic bandages and wound cleansers, make sure the kit includes elastic wraps, plenty of heavy gauze pads, and a good waterproof tape. Be sure to throw your first aid kit into a dry bag before tossing it into your boat.

Emergency Bag

Most of us never think we are going to get stranded out for the night, and though rare, it happens. If you are going to be fishing in a remote area where you can't easily walk out, an emergency bag is a good piece of insurance to bring along. Some food, a headlamp, and some extra clothing can make

Ken Whiting uses his first aid kit dry bag to store his valuables with the idea that no one steals someone's first aid kit. He admits to having once inadvertently and successfully tested his theory at a Florida beach.

what would otherwise be a miserable experience into a tolerable adventure. In cold weather, you may want to consider placing something in your pack to assist you in starting a fire.

Spare Paddle

No matter how well-built your paddle is, there is always a chance it could break or be lost. A spare paddle is simply a must if you are fishing in areas that don't leave you with any options other than paddling home. In a group setting, not every angler needs to have a spare paddle, but there should be at least one spare per group.

Paddle Floats

Paddle floats provide the opportunity to re-enter a capsized sit-inside kayak without anyone's help. The paddle float

attaches to your paddle blade and allows the paddle to be used as an outrigger to stabilize the boat as you get back in. Although they have the potential of being useful, they require training and practice to use. The better option is to avoid paddling alone, so you always have a buddy who can support your kayak while you re-enter.

Bilge Pumps

Kayak bilge pumps are mostly manual, hand-held models. They are only necessary for sit-inside kayaks, which will swamp if they capsize. If you paddle a SINK and venture into waters too deep to wade to safety, you should carry a pump.

If you're going to rely on a cell phone for communication, make sure the batteries are charged and that you have service in the area.

Communication Devices

Communication devices are tools that can help you stay in contact or help manage difficult situations. Of course, they're also great for calling others in your party to see if they're having any luck where they are, or to brag about the fish that you just landed. There are several communication devices available to the kayak angler.

CELL PHONES

Cell phones are a great item to have along. Make sure the batteries are charged and you have adequate cell coverage everywhere you'll be going. Keeping a cell phone dry is a challenge, so you'll want to carry them in a quality dry storage container of some sort. There are even small dry bags designed specifically for cell phones that let you use them while they stay protected inside. Keep in mind that even the slightest amount of moisture can wreck a phone.

VHF RADIOS

An important piece of safety equipment when traveling any distance on the ocean or on very large lakes is a handheld VHF radio, because it can reach other boats in the area, as well as the Coast Guard. You can also listen to an up-to-date weather report. Something to note about VHF radios

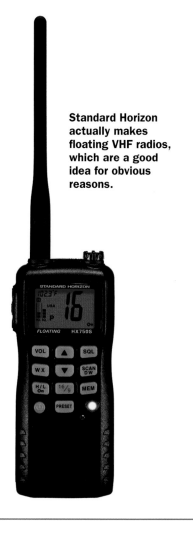

Standard Horizon actually makes floating VHF radios, which are a good idea for obvious reasons.

is that there is a strict and established protocol for their use, which is designed to reduce channel overcrowding and to keep specific channels open to distress calls, so if you want to use one, be sure you know the rules.

Signaling Devices

Signaling devices are used to get attention, and are usually reserved for emergencies.

WHISTLES

A whistle can be heard much more easily and over a greater distance than simply yelling. A small, hand held air horn is even louder. Because they are so small, versatile, and effective, we recommend that you bring one every time you go out in your boat. An easy way to carry it is to attach it to your PFD or stick it in a PFD pocket.

STROBES

A strobe is a very bright, flashing light. Strobes can be attached to the shoulder of your PFD to attract attention at night or in low light, but they should only be activated in an emergency, because on the water, a flashing strobe represents a mayday signal.

FLARES AND SMOKE

Flares at night and smoke during the day can mean the difference between being found or remaining lost. Both are readily available at any marine supply store. There are also dye packs that can be deployed. These dye packs create a huge, brightly-colored cloud on the water's surface to attract the attention of rescue aircraft.

REFLECTORS

You should always carry some sort of reflector along for signaling. A small mirror or a CD will do the job.

Navigation Tools

Navigation tools are pieces of equipment that help you establish where you are on the water and how to get to where you want to be. Basic navigation is something that we all do instinctively (some better than others), and in many cases you won't need any real tools. For example, if you're lost on a lake, you'll know that by following the shoreline one way or another, eventually you'll get back to where you started. Similarly, it is pretty straightforward when fishing on a river. You'll know that if you paddled upstream to begin with, heading downstream on that same side of the river will get you back home. On the ocean or other large bodies of water, if you stick to one shoreline, you can just turn around and head back home at any point. Although navigation tools aren't necessary in these cases, when you start dealing with more complicated marine geography, they quickly become essential. Just buying the equipment isn't enough. Spend some time learning the skills to use these tools and you'll be much more confident when you set out. If you want to fish in more remote areas, you'll want to take a course in navigation. Here is a quick overview of some of the more important navigation tools that you can learn to use.

CHARTS

Nautical charts are basically maps that focus on the marine environment. When buying charts for an area, you'll have to consider what scale is most useful to you. If you intend to get any fishing done, then you probably won't be covering a huge amount of ground, and large-scale charts will be your best option. To carry the charts, you'll need a waterproof chart case.

In areas prone to fog, a chart and compass can be your best friends.

COMPASSES

The magnetic compass is another key navigation tool, but of course, they're only useful if you know how to use them. The best compasses for kayak fishing are hand held and waterproof. There are also deck mounted models available, but they tend to get in the way when mounted on the forward deck.

TIDE AND CURRENT TABLES

Tides and currents can both have profound effects on sea conditions. Happily, both tides and tidal currents can be predicted with reasonable accuracy using tide and current tables, along with the appropriate marine charts.

GPS UNITS

Handheld global positioning system (GPS) units are incredible pieces of technology that can tell you where you are to within a few feet. Data from satellites is used to triangulate your location. Some even have charts built into the unit, which will show you exactly where you are on the map. GPS units are very handy for locating specific fishing locations and mapping out routes to those special places. They're also pretty nice to have when the bite is on, should you stay out a little later than planned and darkness sneaks up on you. When you're focused on the fish, it's easy to get disoriented and a GPS will help you get back to your vehicle.

Basic units are relatively inexpensive and very compact. The only problem with GPS units is that they rely entirely on batteries. Like any other piece of electronic equipment, they are subject to failure in the field. For this reason, you don't want to ever be solely reliant on them. If navigation tools may come in handy, bring a reliable backup, like a compass and chart.

Many fish finders now come equipped with GPS, which means one less piece of gear that you need to remember to bring, but the other option is a handheld GPS.

CHAPTER 2

outfitting your kayak

ONE OF THE GREATEST THINGS about kayak fishing is the opportunity kayaks provide for customization. Most base model fishing kayaks now come with enough outfitting so that you can simply take them directly from the store to the water for some fishing. But it probably won't be long before you'll want to upgrade some of the outfitting or move some things around.

From the outset, it's important that you know that there is no correct way to outfit your kayak. Every type of fishing and every angler will have different needs and ideals, so rather than tell you how to outfit your kayak in this section, we're going to let you know about the outfitting options that are out there and let you decide what will work best. Something that we can almost guarantee is that your outfitting will evolve over time, as you learn what works and doesn't work for you, and as you discover new ideas from other kayak anglers. In fact, this is one of the best reasons to participate in kayak fishing tournaments or other events; they provide a great opportunity to share ideas.

Although you will ultimately need to make your own outfitting decisions, to provide a bit more guidance, at the end of this chapter we've asked pro kayak anglers from around North America to share their outfitting systems with us, along with the reasons why they outfit their kayaks that way. You'll also find more outfitting information in the feature regional fishing articles in the Freshwater Kayak Fishing and Saltwater Kayak Fishing chapters.

A comfortable seat will have a high back, a heavily padded seat, and adjustable straps that clip forward and behind the seat.

Accessories

Seats

Sit-inside kayaks come with prefabricated seats installed and ready to use. A few models of sit-on-tops come equipped with a backrest, but most don't have anything more than the contoured seat pan. Although you can use these kayaks as they are, you can expect a mutiny from your butt and lower back within a short period of time. A simple back band that supports your lower back is an inexpensive and effective solution. However, the best seats will have foam for padding and high backrests that are fully adjustable and quite comfortable. Many of these types of seat will also have added features such as rod holders and detachable storage packs.

It's important to know that most seats designed for fishing kayaks are largely designed to make sitting comfortable and are not necessarily designed to hold your body in a good paddling position. Since you'll be spending a large part of your time sitting and casting, this certainly isn't a bad thing, but you should be aware of how you need to be sitting in a kayak when you're paddling so that you can adjust your seat for it. Good posture in a boat will allow you to paddle more comfortably, promote more efficient strokes, and help you avoid back pain.

The ideal position for paddling a kayak is to sit up straight with your feet resting against the foot pedals or in the foot wells so that your knees are bent and somewhat splayed out. A good seat will have adjustable straps that can be tightened to promote this position. Even with a good seat, some anglers have trouble sitting upright in their kayak without some level of discomfort. This is usually a case of having hamstrings that are too tight. Most anglers we know probably wouldn't adhere to a specific stretching routine, nor do they show much interest in yoga. However, it is important to note that improving your flexibility will make sitting in a kayak a lot more comfortable. So it is worth at least taking a minute or two to do some toe touching (or as close as you can get!) at the put in.

Rod Holders

Rod holders are one of the most valuable accessories for a fishing kayak. They let you easily carry multiple rods, and they keep them all out of the way, so you can paddle unencumbered and still take quick action when you sight a fish. They also offer you the opportunity to troll as you paddle along. Although many current fishing kayaks come equipped with one or more rod holders, there's a good chance that you'll want to add rod holders (which we look at how to do

RAM mounts have a ball base to which the mounted rod holder attaches. Scotty mounts have a receiver that the mounted rod holder fits into.

in the "Installing Accessories" section of this chapter). When doing so, you'll need to decide on the type of rod holder you'd like to use, where you'd like it positioned, and how many you'll need. Obviously, how you'll be using your rod holder is what makes this decision. Does it need to place the rod at an angle suitable for trolling? Will you be setting out multiple baited rods? Or are you simply looking for a place to store your rod while you paddle?

Regarding the positioning of the rod holder, there is no "right" way, simply personal preference. With that said, in our opinion the rod holders are best installed behind your seat, in easy reach. Having as little equipment as possible in

the front of the kayak allows the most freedom while fishing. It's also nice to have the rods in the back and out of the way should you fall out of your kayak and need to perform a deep-water re-entry. In the special outfitting feature at the end of this chapter, you'll learn how some of the top pro kayak anglers use rod holders on their kayaks.

There are three common types of rod holders used by kayak anglers, all of which work well. The standard, flush-mount rod holder commonly seen in powerboats is the most basic type of rod holder. The hollow interior of kayaks makes mounting these holders quick and simple. The models intended for use in kayaks all come with the interior

end capped and sealed, but some models intended for boats are open on the end, allowing any water splashing up onto the kayak to enter. Needless to say, this is not ideal and you will want to cap them. The only downside to this type of rod holder is the fact that your reel is sitting on the deck of the kayak and is much closer to the water. This isn't a huge deal in freshwater, but it will take its toll on your equipment if you're fishing in saltwater. Some kayak anglers have used their creativity to get around this problem by fashioning extenders out of PVC pipe, raising the reel higher off the water.

One of the benefits of flush mount rod holders is that they offer a great place to stow such things as an anchor or Boga grips. Just make sure that whatever you store is tied off to your kayak.

Another common type of rod holder is the adjustable-mounted rod holder, versions of which are made by both Scotty and RAM Mounts. These rod holders will either fit into mounted

Tip As kayak fishing grows in popularity, the number of available accessories keeps growing. Staying involved with regional, online kayak fishing forums is the best way to stay in touch with new developments.

receivers, or in the case of RAM mounts, they can attach to a ball base. There are a number of rod holders now available that fit the same receiver. The type of rod you're using will dictate which rod holder is best. One of the great features of these rod holders is that they can be removed from the kayak when not in use, or during transportation.

A final popular method for storing extra rods is to mount PVC pipe into a milk crate or a small ice chest, which can then be stored in the rear tank well of a sit-on-top kayak. Using this technique, you can carry a variety of rods rigged and ready to go, so you can deal with almost any opportunity that pops up. The disadvantage to this style of rod holder is that your rods are stored farther back in the tank well and you'll likely need to either sit side-saddle or get out of your kayak to access the rods. This isn't a big deal in shallow-water situations, but in rough or deep water it will be more difficult. (For more information about how to install and where to place your rod holders, see the section on Installing Accessories towards the end of this chapter.)

Some people use PVC piping and a milk crate secured in the tank well of the kayak to act as rod holders and storage.

Paddle clips allow the paddle to be stored comfortably and easily along the side of the kayak.

Paddle Holders

Most of the popular sit-on-top fishing kayaks come equipped with some type of built-in paddle holder, which lets you quickly stow your paddle along the side of your kayak and out of the way so that you can cast or fight a fish unimpeded. Some paddle holders use a small piece of bungee cord that loops over the paddle shaft to hold the paddle in place, while paddle clips allow you to simply snap your paddle in and out. Although both styles work well, and we find they come in handy at times, we'll usually just slide our paddles under the cargo bungee cords at the bow of our kayaks. This is a quick and easy way to store your paddle and with practice, it can be done quietly.

If your kayak doesn't have a paddle holder or cargo bungee cords at the bow, both are things that you can install—and which we'll look at later in this chapter. Something to keep in mind is that if you plan to sit and cast from a side-saddle position in a sit-on-top, then you'll want to set up your paddle holder on your off-side so it is usually out of your way. This would also be the opposite side of the kayak from which you prefer to land fish.

Paddle Leashes

When you're fighting a fish in a kayak, it's easy to lose track of your gear, and the paddle has an uncanny knack of taking advantage of the moment to make its getaway. Once the paddle is in the water, even though it's just a few yards away, you'd be surprised by how hard it can be to locate. Throw a little wind into the equation and that paddle can

A paddle leash attaches your paddle to your boat so you can't lose it while preoccupied, such as when you're fighting a fish.

quickly disappear. To prevent this from happening, the paddle leash attaches your paddle to either you or your boat, and is a good piece of security even if you're using a mounted paddle holder.

Anchors

Anchors for kayak fishing are used in the same way that they are when fishing from a powerboat. You'll either set an anchor to hold yourself in place, or use an anchor to slow the speed at which wind pushes you across the water. There are a couple of different styles of anchor that are common and effective for kayak fishing, depending on their desired purpose and the type of bottom you'll be fishing over.

One of the most common types of anchors used for kayak fishing is the folding anchor. These grapple-hook style anchors have three or four points that fold out when in use and that can be folded up and secured while stowed. These anchors seem to work best on soft bottoms or in heavy vegetation, but they don't work as well on hard or sandy bottoms. As a bonus, the folding anchor can be used in its stored position to simply create drag for a more controlled drift.

A lesser-known type of anchor that works great for kayaks is the Bruce anchor, which resembles a plow and works in much the same way. A 2.2-pound Bruce anchor will securely hold a kayak in most any condition and with any type of bottom, short of solid rock.

For drift fishing (see Chapter 4), there are a number of anchors one can use. The most common techniques involve

The folding anchor is popular with kayak anglers, and works really well on soft bottoms or in heavy vegetation.

dragging some type of weight that won't snag along the bottom, or else using a parachute-style anchor that slows you down by catching water. An 18- to 24-inch diameter parachute will be enough to slow you down in any wind that's safe to fish and paddle; you can find them in marine supply and tackle stores. It's a good idea to get a parachute made from a brightly colored material, so you can easily locate it. This will come in handy when you're battling fish, many of which seem to have an uncanny ability to wrap a fishing line around the trailing drift anchor or its rope.

Whichever type of anchor you use, an important part of the anchoring system is the rope itself. A kayak doesn't require the same size rope that a powerboat anchor uses. A 1/4- to 3/8-inch braided nylon rope will work just fine and if it's a soft, braided nylon, it will be easier on your wet hands. Of course, you'll want to occasionally examine the condition of the rope and its knots because anchor failure can get you in real trouble if it happens at the wrong time. It's also highly recommended that you have a knife handy that is capable of easily cutting through your anchor rope, should the need arise.

ANCHOR SETUP

There are a few other accessories that can come in handy. A small brass clip on the end of the anchor rope works well for securing it to various points on the kayak. It's also a good idea to attach a large, brightly colored float to the rope near the clip, so if you need to release the anchor while fighting a fish, you can relocate it afterwards. For a parachute anchor, this float will also keep the chute near the surface and away from bottom snags. In deeper water or in rough conditions, it may also become necessary to attach a short

A Bruce anchor is stored behind the seat in a flush-mounted rod holder.

In shallow water, some anglers prefer to use a stake-out pole to anchor their kayaks. In this photo, Jason LeValley anchors the stake-out pole off a secure loop on the side of his kayak, but you can also put the stake-out pole through a scupper hole.

length of chain to the anchor to help it find purchase on the bottom.

Once you've decided on a type of anchor, your next decision has to do with how you'll attach the anchor rope to your kayak. There are numerous ways to do so, which range from simply clipping the anchor line to a secure point on your boat, to some more complicated trolley systems that allow the user to anchor from any point along the kayak between the bow and stern. Since we prefer to have as little gear around or

in front of us as possible, we like to clip our anchor line to a pad eye located on the side of the kayak, just behind the seat, but again, this is just a matter of personal preference. For many anglers, the anchor trolley is a key accessory.

A **trolley anchor** is simply a loop of 1/8- to 1/4-inch line with a built-in ring for attaching the anchor line. This loop is then strung out along the side of your kayak and passed through clips, or preferably pulleys, at either end. You can then haul on the line and move

the ring to which the anchor line is attached, to any point along the length of the loop. Of course, you'll then need to tie off the line on some kind of cleat to hold its position. Some people like to rig trolley anchors that go from one end of the kayak to the other, while other anglers prefer to set up the trolley system from the midpoint of the kayak to the stern, so they don't have the extra line up front for things to get tangled in. The great advantage of this trolley system is that in current and wind you

In this photo, Chrystal Murray uses an anchor trolley system that runs the line alongside her kayak from the midpoint to the stern, with the line passing through clips instead of pulleys.

can control the position of your boat while it's anchored. The disadvantage to the trolley system is that its ropes running down the sides clutter up the kayak and create an opportunity for you or your gear to get entangled. For more information about using a trolley anchor, see Chapter 4.

Whether you're using a trolley anchor system, or simply clipping your anchor line to a secure point on your kayak, the storage of your anchor is an important consideration. It needs to be located somewhere that is easy to access and yet out of the way. The anchor line also needs to be clear of obstructions

Take your eyes off the lingcod for a moment and note Shimano's Bristol Bay live bait tank in the rear tank well, with the attached rod holders.

Kayak Kevin (Kevin Whitley) uses a trolley anchor. In this photo you can see the anchor line passing through the trolling clip up at the bow. The anchor line has a buoy attached so that he won't lose it if he has to quickly break free of the anchor.

that will hinder the deployment of the anchor. With an SOT, this can be accomplished by placing the anchor and extra rope towards the front of the rear tank well or in a milk crate.

Live Bait Tanks

Although soft plastic baits are getting better and better, live bait is still one of the most effective ways to catch fish. The challenge for a kayak angler is keeping the live bait alive. You have a few options to choose from. You could simply bring along a bait bucket, which you could either drag behind your kayak or store in your back tank well and keep refreshing the water. Another good option is to get yourself a bait tank with a battery operated aerator or recirculating pump. Shimano recently released a kayak fishing portable live

well called the Bristol Bay, which fits great into the rear tank wells of most sit-on-top kayaks, and even has three rod holders integrated into the bag. If you're more of a make-it-yourself person, a quick online search will turn up some how-to articles on making your own live bait tank.

Depending on where you live, Scotty's Trap-Ease crab and prawn trap roller might be a good option.

Howard McKim installs a fish finder.

Fish Finders and Depth Sounders

Although not an essential piece of equipment for kayak fishing, more and more fish finders and depth sounders are finding their way onto kayaks—and for good reason. One of the few drawbacks of fishing from a kayak is that you have a very low vantage point. This means that both fish and bottom features will be more difficult to see, and a fish finder will help out with both. If you're interested in rigging your kayak with either, you'll want to find the smallest units possible to get the job done. The transducers can be mounted inside the hull using an epoxy or heavy-duty silicon sealant/adhesive. As long as there is no air between the transducer and the plastic, the signal will be very good. The other option is to mount the transducer on the outside of the hull. The downside of doing this is that the transducer will create drag and is very prone to snag on sea grass or your fishing line when you're fighting a fish. It's for these reasons that most people prefer to mount the transducer inside their kayak. With that said, boat manufacturers are responding to the anglers' needs, and some boats now have recessed areas by the scupper holes designed specifically so the transducers can be mounted outside the kayak and remain flush to the hull to prevent snagging and excess drag. The line going to your transducer then passes up through the scupper hole and directly to the main body of the fish finder—a very cool solution which avoids imbedding your transducer into a pool of goop!

To power standard fish finders, you'll need some sort of rechargeable 12V source kept in a waterproof container. You could use a 12V battery, a bank of eight AA rechargeable batteries, or even two 6V batteries. To keep the battery(s) dry, you'll use a dry box, dry bag or even a Tupperware container, which should be stored inside a sit-on-top kayak or in a waterproof compartment of a sit-inside.

The main unit should be placed on the deck of your kayak, in a position where you can easily see the screen and work the controls. Although you could mount the unit directly to the kayak, the most convenient and versatile mounting system usually involves the use of a Scotty or RAM mount designed specifically for the job. For more information about installing fish finders, see the "Installing Fish Finders" segment towards the end of this chapter.

As a final note, many fish finders will come with GPS—a worthy upgrade for almost any kayak angler. Even if you don't use the GPS all that often, it's a great piece of safety gear if there's any chance of getting caught in fog or darkness. GPS also offer the benefits of being able to mark hot fishing locations and telling you your traveling speed.

Thigh Straps

Thigh straps are an extra that provide added control for sit-on-top kayaks and only need to be considered for paddling in more challenging conditions, such as when paddling out through surf or in river situations with strong current. For this reason, most kayak anglers will never need thigh straps.

Each thigh strap clips to the kayak behind the seat and up at the feet. In order for them to be effective, they need to offer a snug fit, with your legs splayed out to the side. Because you're looking for a snug fit, padded thigh straps are worth investing in, although in a pinch, you can create basic thigh straps with a couple of cam straps.

Thigh straps provide the paddler with a lot more control over the kayak, but they aren't necessary for most kayak anglers.

All anglers have their own tricks. Brendan uses his mounted fillet board to take care of the dirty work on the water and keep his fish camp clean... and bear-free.

Rudders

Although this may come as a surprise, kayak rudders were not designed to make the boat turn. They're designed to help your kayak "track"—which means travel in a straight line.

Most of the fishing kayaks over 12 feet now come with a molded-in rudder mount in the stern, although there may not actually be a rudder. If the boat does have a rudder mount but no rudder, you can have one installed if you decide that you need one.

Rudders flip down from their stored position on deck by means of haul lines found along the side of the kayak. Unlike skegs, rudders swivel side to side and are controlled by foot pedals. The downside of rudders is that you can expect them to add $150 to $200 to the cost of your kayak, and they are subject to more damage than any other part of your boat.

Pontoons / Outriggers

Pontoons attach behind the seat, and like training wheels for a bike, they provide a huge amount of stability to the kayak. They only really make sense to bring along if you like to stand up in your kayak while fishing, which can be appealing if you're fly fishing or sight-casting.

Packing Your Kayak

ONLY EXPERIENCE will teach you the best way to pack your kayak for the greatest efficiency for your style of fishing. When starting out, just remember to keep close at hand the things that you're going to want quick access to. You don't want to have to search for things like flies and lures, water bottles, or your net. Also keep in mind that certain areas will be inaccessible when you're on the water and will require that you land and get out of your kayak to gain access. These less accessible spots are great places for things like foul weather gear, a first aid kit, or an emergency kit.

One fairly popular piece of equipment for packing a sit-on-top kayak is the milk crate. A milk crate fits in the rear tank well of most common fishing style SOT kayaks. They can be strapped down very easily and provide quick access to a lot of different gear.

Anything that can't get wet will need to be stored in a dry bag, and any loose gear that can sink should be tied to the kayak or your PFD.

A few times out on the water and you'll quickly learn the art of packing your boat. As you gain more experience, you will undoubtedly find yourself shifting the gear around to suit your style. And just when you think you've discovered the best system, you'll run into someone who has an even better idea. This is one of the great things about kayak fishing tournaments. They provide you with the opportunity to see what other people are doing and get ideas that will help you make the most of your time on the water. The most important thing to remember is to try to distribute your gear evenly around the boat. An even weight distribution will help you get the most performance from your kayak.

Dry Stowage

Most kayaks have some sort of built-in dry storage. For a sit-on-top, it's the entire interior of the kayak; for a sit-inside, it's a compartmentalized area in the front and/or rear portions of the kayak. Although these compartments are supposed to be waterproof, there has yet to be designed a kayak storage compartment that doesn't experience

Most sit-on-top kayaks have big enough tank wells in the back to carry everything that you want easy access to. In this photo, Dean Thomas uses a milk crate for most of his fishing tackle and gear, as well as a cooler bag for drinks and snacks.

some leakage. The most common causes of water penetration are waves splashing over the hatches, or the kayak momentarily submerging while traversing large waves. Store anything that needs to stay dry in waterproof containers in the storage compartments. Dry bags work really well, as do hard-shell dry cases such as Pelican boxes. We often see new kayakers using common sandwich type or zip-lock baggies to store their cell phones or cameras and it has cost them on more than one occasion. Go ahead and splurge on the real deal. Get yourself a quality dry bag or box.

Installing Accessories

ONE OF THE COOL THINGS about getting into kayak fishing is rigging your boat. Nothing helps beat the winter blues better than tinkering with your kayak and dreaming of the coming spring. Polyethylene kayaks are easy to work on with basic tools. The only tools you'll need that may not be found in your typical garage are a variable-sized hole saw and a pop rivet tool. These are easy to find and fairly inexpensive to acquire.

Before getting right into it, it's important that you understand from the outset that this segment is designed as a general guideline for installing accessories. Before beginning any installation on your kayak, do your research and make sure you know what you are doing, as installing accessories will likely cause permanent damage to your boat and will void any warranty associated with your kayak.

Fastening Options

When attaching things to your kayak, such as rod holders, paddle clips, pulley systems, eyelets, etc., you have a number of different options. You can use nuts and bolts with washers, or you can use screws, rivets or well nuts. In general, locking nuts, washers, and bolts are the best for attaching anything that will have to take a load (such as a rod holder), but these will be difficult to use if your kayak doesn't allow access to its interior. If this is your situation, rivets are your best bet if the item will be load bearing. When using rivets, be sure to get the type that flare out equally all the way around to more evenly disperse the load. They are often called aircraft rivets, and they aren't easy to find, but they are worth the effort because they do a much better job than standard rivets. You probably won't find them at your local hardware store, but you should find them at your local kayak fishing shop. If the item you're fastening is not load bearing, screws are your easiest option. Keep in mind that the larger the screw, the better it will hold in the kayak. The other option is to use well nuts. Well nuts are convenient because they naturally form a waterproof seal. On the downside, they will leave a gaping hole if they pop out.

On a final note, everything that gets mounted to your kayak should get a liberal application of silicone sealant. The excess silicone can be removed with WD-40 and a rag.

Installing a Flush-Mount Rod Holder or Receiver

Earlier in this chapter, we looked at the different rod holder options and the types of questions you need to ask yourself in order to decide which rod holder(s) are best to install and whereabouts you should place them. Remember that as a general rule, it's a good idea to keep the front of your kayak as clear as possible. In particular, your rod holder shouldn't get in the way of your paddling, so if you're going to install one up front, make sure it's far enough forward to be out of the way while you're paddling. Now we're going

No matter how many times you do it, you'll still get the butterflies when you drill a big hole into a new boat.

to look at how to install a flush-mount rod holder or a flush-mount receiver for mounted rod holders.

First things first—you need to choose a location that is as flat as possible. You'll then use the bottom of the rod holder or receiver to trace a circle on your kayak, which then gets cut out using a drill bit, a hole saw, or a Dremel. Before drilling, double check to make sure that the hole is in the right spot and that it is the right size—and then triple check! Make sure to drill well inside your lines at first, as you want the rod holder/receiver to fit tight. You should expect to need to trim the edges of the hole to make it fit tight and flat against the deck of the kayak.

Once you've got it in place, mark the screw holes. If you're using screws (which are an option since a flush-mount rod holder or receiver won't really be load bearing) you'll drill the holes out with a drill bit that is smaller than the screws you'll be using so that the screws have plenty of plastic to bite into. If you're using nuts and bolts, you'll need to drill the holes to be the right size for the bolt. You're now ready to mount the piece.

Before screwing or bolting the mount or receiver to your kayak, put a good dose of silicone or marine adhesive like "GOOP" on it. You'll then tighten the screws or nuts and bolts and let the silicone (or adhesive) dry.

Installing Fish Finders

By Mark Ezell

Depending on where you fish, a fish finder might be one of the best additions to your kayak. As manufacturers are learning that a huge number of anglers consider the fish finder to be an essential piece of gear, they're coming up with innovative design features that are simplifying the whole installation process. Some kayak manufacturers even offer their boats with fish finders pre-installed.

Most anglers will have to install fish finders themselves, and the following method will help them do so. Before going any further, it's important that you read and understand the manufacturer's instructions for installing the particular fish finder that you've chosen. It's also important that you know that some of the steps involved with this installation will likely void your kayak warranty. If in doubt, get help from someone who has been through the process already, because once you've drilled holes in your kayak, those holes are there to stay.

MOUNTING THE TRANSDUCER

Turn the kayak over and find the flattest area of the hull. You will want to mount the transducer on the inside of the hull close or next to the scupper

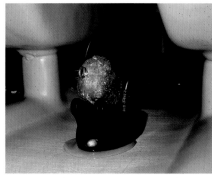

The transducer is embedded in GOOP and a weight is placed on top while it sits still and dries for 24 hours.

holes (the strongest area of a hull, with the least amount of flex), where you can easily reach it. Using emery cloth (150), lightly sand to rough up the area where you are going to mount the transducer. Wipe area clean with a rag. Most manufacturers recommend using a two-part, slow cure epoxy. This works well on a hard surface, but most kayaks area made of plastic and are flexible. "Marine GOOP" is a silicone-based adhesive; it will give and stretch with the bumps of the road, waves, and other movements.

Using Marine GOOP, cover the bottom of the transducer, with no air bubbles in the GOOP. (Use an amount about the size of a quarter for the transducer shown. Your brand may require more GOOP). With your kayak sitting level, place the transducer on the area, pressing down and moving it from side to side just a little bit until it is all the way down against the hull. Now place a weight on top of the transducer, let it dry for 24 hours and make sure that the transducer doesn't move during that time.

MOUNTING THE DISPLAY UNIT

Before mounting your fish finder, mount any rod holders first and then select an area suitable for your display unit.

1. Once you've located a suitable area for the display unit, you'll then drill a hole that is just big enough to fit the plugs through.

2. Using a rubber stopper (which you should be able to find at any hardware store) you will now make a grommet. Start by cutting the stopper in half.

3. Now cut two grooves about 1/8" deep all the way around and 1/8" apart, and then cut out the chunk in between to make a trough in the stopper.

4. Drill two or three holes in the stopper (depending on the unit you have), using a drill bit that is just slightly bigger than the cable, and then slice the stopper from the outside to the holes from different sides.

5. Pull the cables through the hole in the deck and put them into the grommet. You'll then use a screwdriver to work the grommet into the hole. You're now ready to mount the base, which will be strongest if you use nuts and bolts.

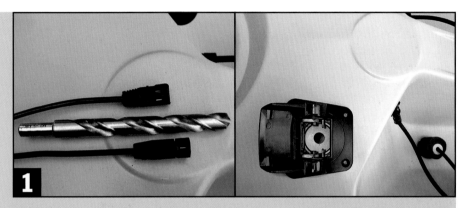

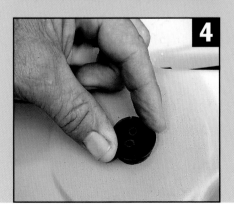

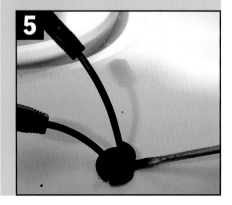

BATTERIES

Your unit's user manual will tell you what power source it requires, but most fish finders will use a 12-volt, rechargeable, sealed lead-acid battery (7-amp-hour). It's also important to get a floating charger, which will turn off when your battery is fully charged.

MOUNTING THE BATTERY BOX

A waterproof box, such as a Pelican box, works great for holding your battery. The following technique is a way to semi-permanently mount the waterproof box inside your kayak so that it stays in place, while the battery can be removed at any time.

1. Cut a pool noodle in half (the width of the box) and glue it (GOOP works well) to the bottom of the box. Once it's dry, place the box inside the front of the kayak where you're going to mount it, and then run a felt tip marker along the hull while marking the pool noodles. You'll then trim the pool noodles outside the line so that they sit flush against the hull.

2. To secure the battery in the box, place the battery in the box, cut sections of pool noodle and glue them in the box to form a nest.

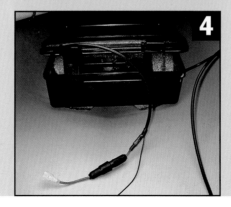

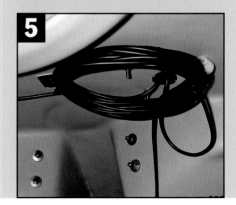

3. Drill a hole in the box for the cable and secure it with a plastic cable clamp. For the area where you'll be gluing down the box, use an emery cloth to rough up the area and then wipe it clean. You can then use GOOP to glue the box (with the battery in the box for weight) down in the hull and let it dry for 24 hours. During the first hour, check every now and then to make sure the battery box is not sliding.

4. On the end of the wire inside the box, attach a watertight fuse and two female flat connectors to attach to the battery.

5. Finally, secure the extra cable out of your way with zip ties and a plastic cable clamp.

Installing Paddle Clips

Paddle clips can come in handy at times, especially if you'll be fishing in windy areas, although it should be known that paddle clips can also get in the way of your paddling if they're improperly placed. As we mentioned earlier, you'll want to position the paddle clips on the opposite side of the kayak from which you prefer to land fish, or where hang your legs over if you fish side-saddle. To ensure your paddle clips won't be in the way of your paddling, it's worth putting your paddle in the clips and finding a spot on the side of the kayak where you want it to go (and where it will fit). The clips should be no closer than three inches to each blade, to make it easy to snap the paddle into place. Of course, the clips can be much closer together than that as well. Once you've chosen a spot, mark the location of the paddle clips. You'll then remove the paddle, duct tape the clips in place and then go for a paddle. If you're not hitting the clips with your hands or paddle, the clips should be in a good spot.

Installing a paddle clip is really pretty simple. Since the paddle clips shouldn't bear any load, you could just screw them in place. Of course, there's always a chance that someone will try to carry your boat by grabbing them, and if they do happen to fail, you'll end up with holes on the side of your kayak where water can easily pour in. So you're better off using locking nuts, washers, and bolts which you'll then waterproof with a sealant (assuming your kayak provides adequate inside access); or you can use rivets or well nuts.

Outfitting with the Pros

Here's how some of the top kayak fishing pros outfit their kayaks. You can be sure that no one has spent more time developing and testing their ideal kayak fishing systems than these guys.

"Bluewater" Jon Schwartz

HOME: San Diego, California

FAVORITE FISH: Striped marlin

FAVORITE KAYAK: Whatever floats!

How many rod holders do you use and where do you place them?

I prefer two flush-mounts in the back. If I use any others, they're just for storage. Half of the time I am traveling somewhere and the kayak is a rental rig, and I end up putting two rods crossways on my lap.

Do you use a fish finder?

Yes, I use Humminbird portables. I love them, they travel well, and I like not having to worry about the interior of my kayak having less rod storage space.

Do you use GPS?

Not yet.

What do you store in your rear tank well?

I have a milk crate that holds a live well. I custom-make my own live well out of a plastic box from any old store. If I am traveling, I usually use dead bait—it's hard to bring a whole bait tank and battery (I've done it but it's a pain)—in which case I just have a cooler in the back. Cooler or live well, I attach a three-rod plastic rod holder from West Marine to it with tape or plastic ties to add to my rod storage.

Do you store gear in any of the hatches?

If I am launching in a place where there is surf, I store some or all of my gear in the front hatch. I'll even break down my rods.

What do you use for a seat?

The Surf to Summit GTS Elite, the one with the high back and grey padding in the middle that looks like the seat of a sports car.

What kind of anchor do you use?

No anchor.

Any other comments about your outfitting?

I am generally a slob, so what I do is, I throw all of my stuff in a nylon backpack and just leave it slung on my legs. That will contain my water, tackle kit, pliers, fish finder until I set it up, camera, suntan lotion, extra leader, etc. I'm not one of those guys who spend a lot of time positioning gadgets on my kayak.

>> Bluewater Jon is a husband, a father and a schoolteacher who started kayak fishing in 2002. He lucked out with some big fish and started a second career documenting his adventures in print and film. He now freelances for fishing and travel magazines and does occasional video shoots for TV shows like National Geographic's Monster Fish. His website is www.bluewaterjon.com.

Mark Pierpont

HOME: Malibu, California

FAVORITE FISH: Calico bass

FAVORITE KAYAK: Wilderness Systems Tarpon 160i

How many rod holders do you use and where do you place them?

I have six rod holders: two front-mounted for trolling and four flush-mount for rod storage.

Do you use a fish finder?

Yes. I use a Humminbird Matrix 37 with built-in GPS.

How do you use the GPS?

Most commonly I use it to determine my speed and drift. The bread crumb feature has saved my butt too, when the fog has rolled in while I'm way out at sea.

What do you store in your rear tank well?

Anything from a bait tank to additional tackle.

Do you store gear in any of the hatches?

In the front hatch: bilge pump, rods for surf launch and reentry, additional tackle, game clip or game bag and mounted battier box for fish finder. Center hatch: marker buoy and fish attractant. Rear hatch: drift chute or sea anchor.

What do you use for a seat?

A customized SeaAir Sports Pacific Angler.

What kind of anchor do you use?

Only on rare occasions will I use a traditional anchor: calm bays, small lakes, or as a means of tying up when doing a river drift. I do use a sea anchor/drift chute to control my kayak in wind conditions.

Do you use a trolley system for your anchor?

No.

Any other comments about your outfitting?

The most common mistake I've seen over the years is overloading a kayak, and not putting enough thought into safety items such as VHF radios, distress whistles, or other signaling devices. Make smart, lightweight, compact and durable equipment choices when outfitting your kayak, but don't skimp on safety.

>> Mark is the Wilderness Systems Kayak Fishing Team Manager. Through his outfitting and guide service, Pacific Fishing Kayaks, he guides kayak fishing expeditions to Baja and mainland Mexico for East Cape Kayak Fishing (www.eastcapekayakfishing.com).

Dean "Slowride" Thomas

HOME: Aransas Pass, Texas

FAVORITE FISH: Red drum, speckled trout

FAVORITE KAYAK: Wilderness Systems Tarpon 160i

How many rod holders do you use and where do you place them?

I use two Scotty fly rod holders directly behind the seat along with two flush-mount rod holders mounted in the kayak behind the seat. I also have a crate with 1 1/4-inch PVC pipe zip-tied to the inside corners for a total of eight spaces to transport rods.

Do you use a fish finder?

No need for a fish finder on the flats of South Texas.

Do you use GPS?

I will use a GPS on multi-day trips to monitor my speed and progress but not so much on day trips around Redfish Bay. Even when I am in new areas, I don't find it necessary to navigate the distance I will be fishing in a day.

What do you store in your rear tank well?

I like to keep things handy that will be used during the course of the day. A soft-sided tackle bag with lure boxes goes bungied in the very back behind the crate. The crate will hold all my essential gear for needs that arise throughout the day: pliers for removing hooks, measuring sticks and electronic scale for keeping me honest, lip gripping device for landing crazy big fish, giant economy-size sunscreen, honey buns (snacks), and a waterproof box with cell phone and fishing license.

Do you store gear in any of the hatches?

The front hatch is a good place for any gear that I may need during the day but which is better stored where it will stay dry and help distribute weight evenly. I keep an extra paddle in case of accident, a well-stocked first aid kit for dealing with hook extraction (from people) and most cuts and scrapes, a dry bag with raingear, and a soft-sided cooler bag for bringing in the catch of the day.

What do you use for a seat?

The Harmony Fishing Seat. Lots of support for long days on the water.

What kind of anchor do you use?

A 3-pound folding grapple anchor with pointed tines. A lot of folding anchors have the spoon-type tines and these will not hold because of the inability to penetrate into the soft bottom. We anchor in strong winds most of the year and the anchor gets a lot of use to help control the boat.

Do you use a trolley system for your anchor?

No. I use a folding anchor attached behind the seat, which I store in my crate.

Any other comments about your outfitting?

I like to keep the deck clear of snags and store most nonessential gear such as the first aid kit, raingear, and extra paddle under the hatch. The items I'll need to get my hands on during the day (small tackle boxes, pliers, lip gripper or net, etc.) go behind the seat.

>> Dean and his wife Jennifer run Slowride Guide Service in Aransas Pass, Texas. Whether you are looking for a fully guided fishing trip or just want to rent a kayak and go exploring on your own, the Thomas duo will take great care of you. Check out their website, www.slowrideguide.com.

Jimbo Meador

HOME: Point Clear, Alabama

FAVORITE FISH: Redfish

FAVORITE KAYAK: Native Watercraft Ultimate 14.5

How many rod holders do you use and where do you place them?

I am mostly fly fishing and sight-fishing so I have my fly rod with the line stripped out in the cockpit, with the rod resting in a groove in the bow within easy reach. I do not put it in a rod holder because I need fast access when I see a fish. If I carry extra rods I store them behind me in a way that makes them easy to access if I need them.

Do you use a fish finder?

I use amber-colored polarized sunglasses. I am sight-fishing in very shallow water. I do use fish finders for other types of fishing.

Do you use GPS?

I do when I need it. I carry a hand-held GPS if there's a possibility I might be traveling in the dark or bad weather, and I use it to save way-points that I might want to return to.

Do you store gear in any of the hatches?

Native boats are slightly different than traditional sit-on-tops. They have bags designed to fit different sections of the kayak so we do not need hatches or tank wells. They also have spray skirts for the bow, stern and midsection so you can adjust to the type of conditions you will be fishing. My rear Watertrail bag includes a tackle bag with built-in rod holders. For an extended trip I would also take an insulated bag for carrying food and drinks. Up front I use a large Watertrail bag for storage of other gear or as a fish bag.

What do you use for a seat?

Native Watercraft's First Class Seating is the most comfortable and versatile seat that I have ever used. It can also be removed and used as a camp chair.

What kind of anchor do you use?

I use numerous types for different situations but when I am poling and sight-fishing I usually stake out with my poling paddle through the ring in my anchor trolley system. If the bottom is too hard to stake out I use a lead ball or a small sea claw anchor that hangs from my stern. The anchor line runs through a fairlead on the stern to a clam cleat within easy reach. All I have to do to stop the kayak is pull the anchor line out of the cleat and drop the anchor.

Do you use a trolley system for your anchor?

Yes. I started experimenting with various systems about 15 years ago and continue to use them now.

Any other comments about your outfitting?

The beauty of kayak fishing is the simplicity of the sport. Keep it simple. I like a kayak that can be very versatile and easily accessorized but that also makes it easy to remove and change the accessories if you plan to use the kayak for multiple fisheries. When I go fishing, I do not want unnecessary clutter.

>> Jimbo Meador has been a commercial fisherman, shrimper and manager of a seafood processing plant; he holds a Coast Guard captain's license for both sail and power vessels up to 100 tons. He has been a professional fly fishing guide and fly casting instructor, and was the Gulf Coast Regional Business Manager for the Orvis Company. He has written for outdoor publications such as *Sports Afield*, *Fly Fishing in Saltwaters* and *Garden & Gun*. Currently, he is Vice President of Kayak Fishing for Legacy Paddlesports, based in Greensboro, North Carolina.

Chad Hoover

HOME: Norfolk, Virginia

FAVORITE FISH: Largemouth Bass

FAVORITE KAYAK: Wilderness Systems Ride 135 and Tarpon 160i

How many rod holders do you use and where do you place them?

I use six: one forward-mounted, two flush-mounts behind the seat and three vertical on the front of my crate. I mount the flush-mounts myself, facing them almost straight back so the rods do not tangle in overhanging trees. This also helps keep them out of the arc of your back cast and lessens the likelihood of entanglement when fly casting.

Do you use a fish finder?

Absolutely. I use the Garmin 300C in conjunction with buoys to mark structure so that I don't have to have the fish finder on all the time. Fish finders continuously "radiate"; the fish and bass can detect it even at the lowest setting.

Do you use GPS?

I use two handheld GPS units—the Garmin 460C and 76CSX—along with mapping software, aerial photography, and topography to develop fishing strategies, and also as the basis for pre-trip planning and post-trip assessment.

What do you store in your rear tank well?

I use a crate system made by 3rd Grip called the Crate Mate Jr. I like this system because it comes with vertical rod holders that have a tool and lure holder built in. The pockets are great for additional soft plastic lures, leader material, small tackle boxes, or any other accessory you may want to organize.

Do you store gear in any of the hatches?

I carry an extra paddle, a first aid kit, batteries, a dry bag with extra clothing and raingear, and my depth finder battery box.

What do you use for a seat?

The Wilderness Systems stock seat.

What kind of anchor do you use?

I use a Bruce or folding anchor for deep water or fast current, a stake out pole or a drag anchor for shallow water, and a lip gripper to clip onto structure like sticks and branches. The stake out poles that I use are the Original StakeOut Pole by CaptDick Enterprises and a golf club with the head cut off. I use several types of drag anchors: a folding anchor secured to the closed position; a window weight; or a water bottle filled with cement with the rope cemented into it. With the lip gripper, I use a lanyard to attach it to my anchor trolley.

Do you use a trolley system for your anchor?

I use an anchor trolley in all fishing situations. I use one continuous loop running fore and aft, with a stainless steel ring in the middle. I use very nice pulleys to make the system operate smoothly.

Any other comments about your outfitting?

- I recommend using a flat black paint designed for plastic to paint your kayak's console. This reduces the glare and makes your depth finder and GPS easier to read, and significantly improves your visual acuity while shallow-water sight-casting.

- I run the bow bungee through a small Nerf ball to make it easier to shove my paddle under for quick stowage.

- I carry a small bowline for wade fishing. I use this with a drag anchor to keep the kayak out behind me when the current or wind would normally force it out in front.

>> Chad grew up hunting and fishing in rural Louisiana and Georgia and is now an active-duty naval officer stationed in Norfolk, Virginia. He developed a passion for saltwater flats kayak fishing while assigned to a search and rescue unit in Corpus Christi, Texas. Chad is an accomplished tournament angler and conducts seminars and clinics throughout the Mid-Atlantic and Southeast. He is a member of the Wilderness Systems Kayak Fishing Team and author of the new book *Kayak Fishing for Bass,* from The Heliconia Press.

"Kayak Kevin" Whitley

How many rod holders do you use and where do you place them?

I use four flush-mounted rod holders, one on each corner of the boat to cover every angle whether I am drifting or anchored. I use vertical rod holders on my crate to keep them from scraping the pilings when fishing around the Bay bridges.

Do you use a fish finder?

No, but I constantly bug those who do: "What do you see now? See anything yet? How deep is it?"

Do you use GPS?

No, I use dead reckoning with maps, charts, and a compass.

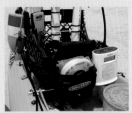

Kevin rigs a suspended crate to keep it drier.

What do you store in your rear tank well?

I rig my crate above my tank well for an extra tier of dry storage where my VHF radio, snacks and other daily essentials are stored. In the well I store bait, water bottles and stuff that can get wet.

HOME: Norfolk, Virginia

FAVORITE FISH: Bull red drum with big stripers a close second

FAVORITE KAYAK: Ocean Kayak Drifter 12.5-foot and a Prowler 15 if I am in a hurry

Do you store gear in any of the hatches?

I carry an extra paddle, a cooler in the summer, empty water bottles and Monster cans.

What do you use for a seat?

Surf to Summit low-back seats for fishing and a high-back Surf to Summit Expedition seat for touring.

Kevin's rock anchor.

What kind of anchor do you use?

For anchoring in the sand, I use the standard grappling style with the spoon blades. The spoons dig into the sand and pull out easy. I do a lot of structure fishing around and over the pilings and rock islands of the bridges and tunnels in the Chesapeake Bay. I anchor up with a kayak-size wreck anchor. It's a 20-ounce lead sinker with an eye loop and four thin metal rods in the weight. The rods grab the rocks and are easily bent straight and retrieved.

Do you use a trolley system for your anchor?

Yes. My trolley system is easy. I use two separate trolleys from mid-ship to the bow and stern. I use carabiners for pulleys and the rope slider.

Any other comments about your outfitting?

I keep it real simple but precise. Everything is in the same place on any of the boats I use regularly. I like to keep my deck clear when hunting big fish or they will kick everything out.

>> In 2006 Kevin set his sights on the Virginia saltwater fishing tournament's Expert Angler award, which requires catching six different trophy-size fish in a year. In that year, Kevin was the first kayak angler to achieve the Expert Angler award and in 2007 he became the first to achieve it twice.

Jeffrey Goudreau

HOME: Queen Charlotte Islands, British Columbia

FAVORITE FISH: I enjoy catching Pacific Halibut the most... I love the idea that this fish can break your legs with a tail whack...

FAVORITE KAYAK: Ocean Kayak Trident 15

How many rod holders do you use and where do you place them?

I like my rod holders in a few spots. I use two Scotty rod holders in the head of the pit, one facing each direction. I also have a RAM ball-mount for a holder that's close to my knee on either side so if it's a style that needs faster reaction to get proper hook set, I can get to it fast—and also for drifting bait and sitting sideways as I'm drifting.

Do you use a fish finder?

Yes. Humminbirds.

Do you use GPS?

Nope.

What do you store in your rear tank well?

Nothing.

Do you store gear in any of the hatches?

I sometimes have huge breaks to paddle through to get to the beaches after the day's done, if my timing of the tides wasn't right or I needed to get in because of weather. At this time I need to store everything in order to keep it, because it can easily cause me to flip. The Rod Pod in the Trident is great for this—that way in big swells I don't have to jump all the way up front to store things. I usually have lots of expensive camera gear to store inside too.

What do you use for a seat?

I'm not that picky. I'm an easy-to-please dude. Sometimes I forget my seat altogether 'cause it's not important to me.

What kind of anchor do you use?

I use various sizes depending on what I'm doing—10-pound balls from the downrigger for windy sand-flat fishing, drift chutes for various bottom structure during wind or to maximize my slack tides, and just plain old 4-pound folding ones for anchoring in relaxed areas.

Do you use a trolley system for your anchor?

Nope. My boat came with a factory installed trolley, but I just don't use it. I simply clip my anchor to the rings on my boat.

Any other comments about your outfitting?

I like things spread out, but not unorganized. I'm not up on a lot of the new products out there, like all the tackle storage systems. Because at any time I can hook into a fish over 200 pounds, I like to bring only what's necessary. This way, if I lose gear from a wrestling match, I'm not too bummed. Also, I need things linked to the boat, so I have everything attached with a dog clip and a perfection loop.

>> After seven years of guiding in some of Canada's most pristine fisheries, Jeff learned about kayak fishing on the Internet and immediately fell in love with the idea. Now an Ocean Kayak Pro Staff member, Jeff runs Extreme Kayak Fishing Expeditions and takes anglers on specialized kayak fishing/camping trips in the Queen Charlotte Islands. For more information, visit www.CanadianKayakAnglers.com.

Howard McKim

HOME: Ketchikan, Alaska

FAVORITE FISH: Lingcod

FAVORITE KAYAK: A 15-foot or longer sit-on-top. I currently use the Ocean Kayak Trident 15

How many rod holders do you use and where do you place them?

Two or three rod holders, all behind the seat. I like a clean deck up front, without any obstructions. I like the tube style that keeps the reels up out of the waves. I troll with the rod in my lap, so I never have the active rod in a rod holder. They're only for storage.

Do you use a fish finder?

I like to. We fish so deep here it's nice to know the depth. All I need to know is how deep it is. I have a variety of units, but have had the best success with Lowrance units.

Do you use GPS?

Sometimes. I usually have one, but it's mostly for emergency or dense fog. Too many people rely on GPS and cell phones. Be sure it's only for backup.

What do you store in your rear tank well?

Fish. I try to keep it empty except for fish. Nothing worse than putting fish inside a kayak.

Do you store gear in any of the hatches?

I usually carry an emergency dry bag with basic survival stuff like a bivy sack and fire starters and such. It's good to know you can spend the night.

What do you use for a seat?

I like SeaAir Sports seats. Excellent back support.

What kind of anchor do you use?

No anchors for me because the water is too deep for them to be of use.

Any other comments about your outfitting?

I like to keep it simple. I see a lot of over-outfitted kayaks. The more time you spend out there, the less gear you'll consider necessary. Take a few basic things and keep them in the exact same place every time. Then when you hook the big one, you can focus on the fight.

>> Howard McKim is Southeast Alaska's number-one kayak fishing guide and the owner of Ketchikan Kayak Fishing (www.yakfishalaska.com).

Chris LeMessurier

HOME: Berkley, Michigan

FISHING GROUNDS: Inland lakes, rivers, the Great Lakes and their tributaries.

FAVORITE FISH: King (chinook) salmon, northern pike, smallmouth bass, largemouth bass

FAVORITE KAYAK: Wilderness Systems Tarpon 140

How many rod holders do you use and where do you place them?

I have three to four rod holders on my kayak at any given time. I use RAM rocket launchers behind my seat and either a RAM 117U or RAM fly rod holder in my cockpit.

Do you use a fish finder?

Yes. I use a Humminbird 363.

Do you use GPS?

Yes. My fish finder has a built-in GPS, which kills two birds with one stone. This arrangement helps to free-up valuable space in the cockpit.

What do you store in your rear tank well?

A small dry bag containing sunscreen, a first aid kit, and a towel.

Do you store gear in any of the hatches?

My Roleez wheels and homemade cart (only when beach launching).

What do you use for a seat?

I prefer a comfortable seat with a gel cushion bottom.

Yakpads makes a great seat bottom, but the best I've found so far is the Skwoosh Voyager.

What kind of anchor do you use?

I use a 4-pound cannonball, the ones normally used on downriggers. It works well to hold my kayak in place, yet doesn't get caught on the bottom.

Do you use a trolley system for your anchor?

No. I attach carabiners to the bow and stern handles. The anchor line runs through the carabiners, into the cockpit, and is locked off in a cleat. This system allows me to drop one or both of the anchors with only one free hand.

Any other comments about your outfitting?

I have come full circle when it comes to rigging or loading a kayak for fishing. There are hundreds of interesting gadgets and toys designed for the kayak angler. When I first began this sport, years ago, I had to have them all. Now I've gone back to the basics and my rigged kayaks look kind of bare. My philosophy is "less is more."

>> Chris is a member of the Hook 1 Crew, the Wilderness Systems Kayak Fishing Team and the Michigan Kayak Fishing Team (www.MichiganKayakFishing.com).

CHAPTER 3

before hitting the water

Care and Maintenance for Your Kayak and Gear

KAYAKS are extremely simple and low maintenance watercraft, especially when compared to powerboats. However, there are a few ways that you can prolong the life of your kayak and maintain its overall appearance and performance.

One of the most common ways to damage a kayak is to store it improperly. There are a few good ways to store a kayak. You can lean it up on its side, cradle it with hanging straps, or set it on a padded rack that supports the bow and stern. Regardless of how you store it, make sure that you remove any water or extra gear from inside, as the additional weight can cause the hull of the kayak to deform. It's also important that you keep your kayak out of the sun as much as possible. The sun's powerful UV rays will dull its color and make the material more brittle and subject to cracking.

Saltwater can also takes its toll on a kayak and your gear over time, but a simple freshwater rinse will take care of that. Pay particular attention to any metal parts such as rudders and their cables, deck cleats, and any other moving parts such as foot pegs.

Something to note is that it is normal for the hull of plastic kayaks to deform a bit over time, but unless the deformity is major, it should have virtually no impact on your kayak's performance. If the boat is showing serious warping or dents, a little heat will often be enough to return the kayak to its original shape. On a hot day, leaving your kayak in the sun for a little while will often be enough to pop out the dents. If that doesn't work, you can dump some hot water into the kayak and use your hands (don't burn yourself!) to encourage some of the dents to pop out.

With enough force (and it takes a lot), it's possible to crack or puncture a kayak, which is obviously a serious problem. Composite boats with this kind of damage can be repaired quite easily by someone who is experienced in fiberglass work. Plastic boats can be repaired through careful use of a heating source and some spare plastic. It is a good idea to keep any cut-outs or drill bit shavings for future use in any patching jobs that may arise.

Transporting Your Kayak

Not surprisingly, one of the most common questions we field at boat shows, demo days, and kayak symposiums has to do with transporting kayaks. It's a valid concern, because transporting a 10- to 16-foot boat does take a game plan, and it's not something that you want to mess up. Losing a kayak on the freeway is as dangerous as it gets; maybe not for you, but for the other drivers on the road.

There are basically three options for transporting fishing kayaks. You can tie your boat onto a roof rack, tow the kayak in a trailer, or if you have a pick-up, you can simply tie the kayak into the bed of the truck. If you're going to tie the kayak into the bed of your truck, don't forget that in most areas you are required to put a red flag on anything that extends more than four feet beyond the rear of the vehicle. This requirement may vary, so check your state and local regulations to be sure.

The nice thing about trailers is that loading them is generally very easy and you'll usually be able to carry several kayaks at the same time. With some creativity, you can take a trailer designed for a powerboat and make a few small modifications that will allow it to carry kayaks. The downside is trailer storage, registration fees, and maintenance will be required.

Roof racks are by far the most popular method of transporting kayaks and there are models available to accommodate almost any vehicle. Unfortunately, factory installed racks are seldom strong enough to transport kayaks, so you'll need to consider an alternative. The cheapest option is to use simple foam blocks that sit on the roof of your vehicle. You'll then strap the kayak down to your car using cam straps threaded through your vehicle. Although this can do the trick for short trips, the ideal roof racks are those like the ones that Thule (www.thule.com) offers. Thule has rack systems for every type of vehicle as well as ones that are specifically designed for carrying kayaks. They are all designed to be mounted on your vehicle and can be purchased with a mechanism that locks the racks to your vehicle. Another great option for kayak anglers are boat cradles and kayak rollers. Boat cradles mount onto the racks and cup your boat. This holds them in place and spreads the load when you tie the kayak down, which helps prevent deformation of the hull. Kayak rollers have wheels that help you slide the boat onto your vehicle from behind, making loading and unloading easier. Whatever type of roof rack that you use, it's always a good idea to tie bow and stern lines to the front and back of your vehicle to help stabilize the kayak and prevent it from shooting off like a torpedo if you need to brake quickly.

The ideal roof racks are specifically designed for the purpose. Factory-installed racks aren't usually reliable or strong enough.

Carrying Your Kayak

Although there are a lot of benefits to using a plastic kayak, weight isn't one of them. Plastic kayaks tend to be somewhat heavy, which can make carrying a kayak a bit of a pain. The best way to carry a boat from your vehicle to shore is the buddy system, with one person holding the grab loop at each end. Many fishing kayaks come with a grab handle along the side of the boat, for carrying it suitcase style. While this works, you probably won't want to carry your kayak for long distances using this method. If you're alone, it might be best to drag the kayak to the shoreline, but be careful of the type of surface you'll be traversing. Concrete, asphalt, and rocky shoreline are going to take a toll on your boat.

1. Lift the kayak onto your thighs with the cockpit out.

2. Grab the far edge, thumb out, with the hand that is on the same side as the shoulder that the boat will sit on.

3. Use your knee to kick the boat up and roll it onto your shoulder.

4. To recover your paddle, you can use your foot or squat, keeping your back straight.

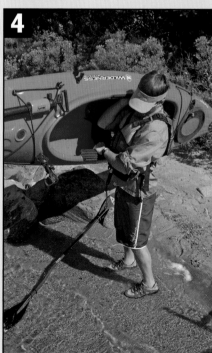

Kayak carts will pack down and store inside most kayaks while you're fishing.

Sit-inside kayaks also offer the opportunity to shoulder-carry the kayak, although getting it onto your shoulder can be a challenge on its own. When doing so, make sure you bend your legs and keep your back as straight as possible. Start by grabbing the close side of the cockpit coaming and then lifting the boat onto your thighs so that the cockpit is facing outwards. You'll then grab the far edge of the coaming, and roll the boat up and onto your shoulder. To put the kayak back down, reverse these steps.

Another great option if you need to carry your kayak any distance is a kayak cart. Kayak carts have two wheels and support the kayak at either the end or in the middle. Most carts pack down on the top deck of a kayak or inside the hull.

Getting In and Out of Your Kayak

The easiest spots to get into and out of your kayak are beaches or flat areas where you can walk your kayak into the water, straddle it, and then sit down. When doing this, one end of your boat will often remain on land, so you may need to push off with your hands. If you push off with your paddle, push directly down the length of the shaft to avoid breaking a paddle blade.

Unfortunately, launch sites aren't always so convenient. In particular, docks and rocky shorelines can be tricky. With a little technique and practice, you'll be able to launch from all sorts of different places. The freedom to launch virtually anywhere is one of the huge advantages of kayak fishing.

If you find yourself needing to launch from a dock, choose the dock's lowest point. The higher the dock, the more chance you have of finding yourself swimming. Start by positioning your

kayak parallel to the dock, and then sit down on the dock beside the kayak seat. Place your paddle close by, so it will be within easy reach once you are in your boat. Next, put your feet in the kayak close to the centerline of the boat for maximum stability. Now turn your body towards the bow of the kayak, securing a good grip with both hands on the dock, and then lower yourself decisively into the seat. It's this awkward transition from sitting on the dock to sitting in the kayak where most of the carnage takes

For awkward or rocky launching sites, float your kayak parallel to shore and use your paddle as an outrigger for support on shore as you get on board.

place, so be quick about getting your butt into the seat. To get out, you can simply reverse these steps.

For awkward or rocky launch sites, the best way to get into your boat is to float your kayak in the water, and then use your paddle as an outrigger for support. Place your paddle at 90 degrees to the kayak, with the shaft resting on the boat just behind the cockpit and the far blade supported on the shore. Grasp the paddle shaft behind your back and squat down beside the kayak. While cheating your weight onto the outrigger, slip your legs into the boat and drop your butt into the seat. You can get out of your kayak on uneven or rocky shorelines using this same technique in reverse, although it will be difficult if you have any waves to contend with.

Something to consider after a long day on the water, particularly if you haven't stood up in awhile, is that your legs may not do everything that you want them to. An all too familiar and funny scene involves an angler stepping out of their kayak and then falling straight back into the water because their legs simply won't respond. Save yourself the embarrassment—take a moment to plan your exit and give your legs a good shake before you hop out.

Using Your Paddle

In the next chapter we'll be taking an in-depth look at the various strokes and paddling techniques, but for now we're going to look at the basics of using a paddle. Not only will this let you make the most of your strokes, but it will help you avoid overuse injuries such as tendonitis in the wrist or elbow.

A kayak paddle should be held with your hands an equal distance from the blades and slightly more than shoulder width apart. A great way to establish the correct hand placement is to position the center of the paddle on top of your head and then grip the paddle so that your elbows are bent at approximately 90 degrees.

Knowing roughly where your hands should be, the next thing to look at is whether or not your paddle has any feather to contend with. Feathered paddles have blades offset at different angles. As one blade pulls through the water, the angle of the other blade allows it to slice through any wind. Feathered paddles are traditional and can make a small difference if you're paddling in an area with high winds, but they are less intuitive to use and by no means essential. You may want to try both feathered and unfeathered paddles and decide on which you prefer. Let's start by taking a look at how to use a feathered paddle, since it is a useful concept to understand whether your paddle is feathered or not.

First off, you need to decide which hand will be your control hand. In general, if you are right-handed, your right hand will be your control hand. Likewise the left hand will be the control hand for left-handed paddlers. This "control" hand keeps a firm grip on the shaft at all times which is why it is also referred to as the "glue" hand. The opposite hand, in contrast, is often referred to as the "grease" hand. The control hand's grip should never change whether you're forward paddling, back paddling, or performing any other stroke. The big knuckles of your control hand should be aligned with the top edge of your paddle blade. After taking a stroke with your control hand side, you'll loosen your grip with your grease hand so that you can rotate the shaft within it. This rotation is necessary to accommodate the feather of your paddle, and lets you place the next blade in the water squarely. This loosening of the grease hand and the rotation of the shaft within it takes place between each stroke.

1. If the right hand is the control hand, it should retain a firm grip, with the big knuckles aligned with the top edge of the paddle blade.

2. The left hand stays loose so that after a stroke is taken on the right, the shaft can rotate in the left hand so the left blade can be planted squarely in the water.

If you're using a paddle with no feather you can get away with not rotating the paddle between each stroke. However it is ideal to use this same technique in a scaled-back way because there is naturally a small amount of rotation associated with paddling. If you don't let the paddle shaft rotate a little in your grease hand, you'll find that wrist doing small curls while you paddle, which can gradually result in an injury or strain.

On a final note, it's important that you keep your control hand grip on the paddle secure, but as light as possible. Certainly don't white-knuckle it. A light grip will let you paddle more comfortably for longer, and is instrumental for avoiding overuse injuries such as tendonitis in the wrist and elbow.

CRAB MAN
ayak Launch
and
Parking Fee
$2.00 per unit *Mgr.*

It's not always going to be an option, but the best kayak launches are sloping beaches where you can pull your kayak out onto the water, then straddle it and hop in.

Choosing a Kayak Fishing Location

If the quick trips after work are the dessert, then the all day trips on the weekends are the full course meal. And planning for those trips is half the fun. Make sure that you watch the weather reports so you know what type of conditions you'll be dealing with, but remember that kayaks allow you the option of launching from places where boaters can't. Take advantage of this asset and you can usually find a protected area to fish, even on the windiest of days. Anywhere you can park your vehicle and access the water without trespassing is fair game. Bridges over creeks or rivers are perfect launch points, as are roadside parks. Given the light weight and durability of today's fishing kayaks, it isn't too difficult to negotiate moderately rough terrain in your quest for under-utilized waters. We've launched our kayaks from a variety of locations that many people would never even consider. Just make sure you identify some obvious landmarks from on the water so that you can find your vehicle at the end of the day when the light is low.

You probably already have a couple of places in mind for your area, but once you get into the sport you'll likely find yourself looking at things a bit differently. Many of our favorite fishing holes were discovered while driving around the countryside. Any time we cross a body of water that appears big enough to accommodate a kayak, we make note of it for further investigation. From there it is simply a matter of using the Internet to search out maps and aerial photos to find out whether or not this piece of water looks interesting enough to warrant an investigatory trip. It isn't exactly pioneering the West, but it does give a sense of exploration.

Of course this is all dependent upon the type of water we're talking about. If it is a piece of flat water, perhaps the arm of a bay estuary or a lake, then the exploration is rather simple. You can drop in and paddle in either direction and be relatively secure in knowing that you can safely explore the area and return to your launch. Moving water will require a bit more planning and preparation. You'll need to learn to judge the flow rate and do a bit more background research on the waterway. Local river guidebooks can be invaluable in determining whether or not the waterway is within your skill level. On lesser creeks you'll need to check the topographical maps to learn whether there might be potential dangers downstream. You'll also need to plan on setting up a shuttle if the flow is too great to paddle back upstream to your launch.

Overnight camping trips are also a viable option for the kayak angler. The storage capacity of today's fishing kayaks allows you to take along plenty of gear for a multi-day trip. Camping gear designed for backpackers is perfect for the kayak camper. Small compact tents, sleeping bags, and even cooking supplies are readily available. This opens up a whole world of fishing possibilities that are unreachable on a day trip. In our modern world of convenience stores and fast food, there is something very satisfying about paddling to a distant shoreline to set up camp and then going out to catch your own dinner.

From a safety standpoint, it's important that we clearly establish the line between recreational kayak fishing (which doesn't require specific training or instruction) and advanced kayak fishing (which requires specialized kayak training). There are three major factors that will dictate whether you're choosing an appropriate kayak fishing location: the type of fish you're targeting, your exposure to wind and waves, and your proximity to shore.

Obviously, the type of fish you're targeting will have a large bearing on what is and is not a good fishing location. For example, the tarpon in Florida offers an amazing challenge to kayak anglers, and there are many inland flats filled with tarpon and appropriate for kayak fishing. On the other hand, kayak fishing for tarpon in deeper water exposed to wind and waves, and in which large sharks are present, is generally not such a good idea. Before even considering it, you should be highly experienced and have a powerboat on hand for safety and support.

With respect to wind and waves, as soon as you venture into water that isn't protected, and/or you travel further from shore than you can comfortably swim, you are entering a new world. You need to protect yourself by getting informed and developing practical kayak rescue skills. The best way to do so is by taking a sea kayaking rescue course. You'll learn to deal with the rough conditions that you may encounter, along with rescue skills necessary for dealing with the situations that may arise. It's simply not appropriate to learn rescue skills by trial and error in rough water conditions.

Unless you are trained in kayak rescue or have a safety powerboat at close hand, you need to choose a kayak fishing location that is sheltered from wind and waves, and you need to stay within swimming distance of shore.

the essential strokes and paddling techniques

BY KEN WHITING

MOST OF THE PEOPLE who get into kayak fishing are anglers looking for a new experience and a way to catch the big one. The idea of developing sound paddling skills is often an afterthought. But make no mistake: better paddlers are better kayak anglers. Period. With solid kayaking skills, not only will you increase the area that you can comfortably fish on a given day and avoid overuse injuries, but you'll be able to follow key fishing structures more effectively and travel more stealthily. There are a ton of other benefits too. You'll be able to control your boat better while fishing in wind. You'll be able to break through ocean surf that others wouldn't consider attacking. If you enjoy trolling, you should know that a good paddler can more effectively monitor and control their trolling speed, especially when you have wind or waves to contend with. Simply put, developing good paddling technique will not only enhance your kayak fishing experience, it will make you a better angler. It's for that reason that you'll find that many of the top kayak fishing pros are taking sea kayaking and whitewater kayaking courses.

Forward Stroke

Although any stroke that gets your kayak moving forward is fine, with a proper forward stroke, you'll be able to get where you want to go more efficiently and with the least amount of wasted effort. The bottom line is that you'll give yourself more fishing time!

Since the forward stroke is the stroke that you'll use 99% of the time, we're going to look at it in a fair amount of depth. In fact, we're going to look at the stroke in three distinct parts: catch, rotation, and recovery.

1. To plant your forward stroke, reach with the blade toward your toes by twisting at the waist.

2. Make sure that as you pull on your stroke, the blade is fully submerged.

3. When the paddle blade reaches your hip, the forward stroke is done, and you can slice your paddle up out of the water.

4. As soon as one stroke finishes, drop the opposite blade into the water at the toes.

5. Notice that the arms move very little as the stroke is pulled through. The power for the stroke comes from torso rotation.

6. By minimizing the movement of your kayak while you paddle forward, it will glide more efficiently through the water, and most importantly, help you avoid startling fish.

Forward Stroke

Catch

The *catch* refers to the moment when your paddle blade is planted in the water. Sitting up straight, with a relaxed grip on your paddle, reach to your toes and plant your blade fully into the water. This reaching action involves both your arms and your shoulders. Do not lean forward at the waist to reach to your toes, but rather twist from the waist. If you're reaching for a stroke with your right blade, you'll push your right shoulder forward while reaching with your right arm. This shoulder-reach causes you to rotate or "wind up" your upper torso and is commonly referred to as *torso rotation*. Torso rotation lets you harness the power of your front and side stomach muscles for your strokes rather than just using your arms. With your body wound up, spear your blade into the water so that the whole blade is submerged. Once that blade is completely in the water, you'll then pull on your paddle and unwind your upper body to drive your boat forward.

One of the most common mistakes is pulling on the forward stroke before the blade is fully submerged in the water. If you're doing this, you'll notice your strokes creating a lot of splash, which means that you're actually wasting energy pulling water past your kayak rather than pulling your kayak forward through the water. To understand this better, imagine that you're planting your paddle in cement when you take a stroke, and then pulling yourself up to the paddle, rather than pulling the paddle back to yourself. The only way this will work is if you have fully and securely planted your whole blade in the water.

Rotation

Once it's wound up, your body is like an elastic band in that you'll have a lot of potential energy at your command. *Rotation* refers to the way you'll use this energy to power your forward stroke.

As described above, after the catch, your body should be wound up and your paddle firmly planted at your toes. You'll now pull on your paddle and drive your kayak forward, using as much of your large torso muscles as possible, rather than relying on your comparatively weak arms to do the work. In fact, a good way to think about this is that your arms are just a supplement to the power of your torso. True power comes from your stomach, side, and back muscles. If you don't believe it, try paddling forward with your arms locked straight at the elbows. Paddling in this manner may seem awkward at first, but you can really get your boat moving—and the only way to do it is with pronounced torso rotation.

Now that you're engaging the most powerful muscles, let's take a quick look at what the rest of your body will be doing. With elbows bent and staying low, pull on the paddle with your arms as you take each stroke. Since your torso will be doing the bulk of the work, the motion of your arms will be quite small. As a general rule,

the more vertical the paddle shaft is while taking a forward stroke, the more power you're getting from it. To get the paddle more vertical, bring your top hand higher and further across your boat. These sprinting strokes are great when you're in a hurry, but they're also very tiring. For general paddling purposes, keep your top hand at about shoulder or chest level. In very shallow water you'll find that you need to lower your top hand a bit and allow the blade to maintain a shallower angle with less of the blade entering the water.

For maximum drive, your legs can also be involved with your forward stroke. By pushing with the foot on the same side that you're taking a stroke you will help transfer more power to your stroke.

Recovery

The *recovery* is the point at which your forward stroke ends and the blade is removed from the water. This happens at your hip, which is earlier than most paddlers expect or practice. When your stroke reaches your hip, slice your paddle up out of the water sideways and get ready for the next stroke, which means unwinding your body past its position of rest and then winding it up in the opposite direction, ready for the next catch of your other blade on the other side.

Now that you have all the pieces for an efficient and powerful forward stroke, try to put them all together as smoothly as possible while keeping your boat as "quiet" as you can. A "quiet" boat has minimal bob from side to side or up and down, and will glide through the water most efficiently.

Notice the active blade is fully submerged and the top hand is at around chin level.

Reverse Stroke

1. The back stroke is planted firmly in the water, just behind your hip and with your upper body rotated towards it.

2. Notice the arms stay in a relatively fixed position. Torso rotation provides much of the power for the stroke.

3. The reverse stroke finishes when your blade reaches your toes.

4. Wind up your body in the other direction before planting the next blade.

5. Plant the paddle fully in the water before pushing on it.

6. Once again, torso rotation provides the real power for your reverse stroke.

Although you might not use the reverse stroke very often, it can come in handy when maneuvering to set up for a cast and in narrow channels.

Not surprisingly, the reverse stroke is just like the forward stroke, only done in reverse. The first thing to know is that you shouldn't rotate the paddle in your hands to use the power face. Your grip on the shaft will remain the same as always, which means you'll use the backside of the paddle for the stroke.

With your top hand held in a relaxed position in front of your body at a level between chest and chin height, plant your blade just behind your hip and push it to your toes. As you plant your blade deeply in the water behind your hip, turn your upper body in the same direction. By rotating towards your paddle like this you can use the power of torso rotation as you did with your forward stroke. After your stroke reaches your toes, wind your body up in the other direction to get ready to drop the next stroke behind your hip on the opposite side.

As a final note, remember to look behind you every few strokes to avoid running into something or someone else! It's easiest to do this by glancing behind you as you plant your stroke.

Using the Reverse Stroke as a Brake

Whether you are approaching a dock, a boat, or paddling over to your buddy to get one of the lures that seems to be working a lot better for him than the ones you have, you're going to need to put on the brakes at some point. You'll do so with a series of short and quick alternating reverse strokes called "braking" strokes. With three short and powerful braking strokes, you should be able to fully stop your kayak from any speed.

1 **2**

Sweep Strokes

Most fishing kayaks are designed to travel well in a straight line and are not designed to turn very much. This means that it will take a few good strokes to turn a fishing kayak around. Sweep strokes are what you're going to use. You can use forward and/or reverse sweep strokes while stationary or when moving. We're going to take a quick look at the technique used for both.

Forward Sweep

1. The forward sweep starts with your body wound up and your paddle planted deeply at your toes, with the shaft held low.

2. Keeping your hands low, sweep an arcing path far out to the side of the kayak.

3. Follow your active blade with your eyes to help incorporate torso rotation into the stroke.

4. Finish your sweep before your paddle hits the stern of your kayak.

The forward sweep stroke is usually used to turn a kayak while stationary or to make small course corrections while traveling forward.

Just like the forward stroke, the forward sweep starts with your body wound up and your blade completely in the water at your toes. It also harnesses the power of torso rotation. Unlike the forward stroke, your hands will stay very low during the sweep and your blade will follow an arcing path as far out to the side of your kayak as possible. To do this, the hand controlling the active blade will reach out over the water while the other maintains a low position in front of your stomach. Your blade will continue on its arcing path until it approaches the stern of your boat. You'll then slice your paddle out of the water before it touches the stern and move to your next stroke.

When you practice this stroke, keep your eyes on the active blade throughout its arc to get the most power from your torso rotation. Following the blade with your eyes will force your upper body to rotate throughout the stroke. Once you've become very comfortable with the forward sweep, you'll be able to keep your eyes on where you're going instead of following the blade. You can also push off the foot pedal on the sweeping-stroke side of the boat, for even more power.

Sweep Strokes

Reverse Sweep

1. The reverse sweep starts at the stern of your kayak, with your head and body aggressively rotated towards it.

2. Keeping your hands low, sweep a wide arc with your paddle.

3. Notice the arms have stayed in a relatively fixed position throughout the stroke, which means torso rotation is providing much of the power.

4. The stroke ends after having swept a full, wide arc.

The reverse sweep is simply a forward sweep done in reverse—and like the reverse stroke, you'll use the backside of your paddle. The reverse sweep is an effective tool for the kayak angler as well. Have you ever been slowly cruising a shoreline, only to see some activity peripherally just behind you? A good reverse sweep on the shoreline side of your boat will stop your forward movement and turn you quickly into position to cast at your prey.

The reverse sweep starts with your body wound up and your blade completely in the water at the stern of your kayak, about six inches away from the hull. In order to put the most torso rotation possible into your stroke, keep your eyes on the active paddle blade. With the blade planted deeply in the water, sweep a wide arc all the way out to the side of your kayak up to your toes. The hand on the side of the active blade reaches out over the water while the other stays in front of your stomach. By keeping your head turning with your active blade, you will encourage good torso rotation and ensure that your body unwinds throughout the whole stroke.

Tip Once you're comfortable with both sweep strokes, try combining the two. A forward sweep on one side, followed by a reverse sweep on the opposite side, is the quickest way to turn a stationary kayak.

Draw Strokes

Draw strokes are used to move your kayak sideways, such as when you want to pull yourself up beside a buddy, a boat, or a dock.

Basic Draw

The draw stroke is a great way to pull up alongside a dock.

The basic draw involves reaching out to the side of your kayak at the hip and pulling water towards you using the power face of your paddle. For the most effective stroke, plant your blade completely in the water, rotate your head and upper body to face your active blade, and hold your paddle as vertical as possible. Getting your paddle vertical requires reaching across your upper body with your top hand. This takes some real balance,

so you might want to start by practicing your draw stroke with your top hand held lower and in front of your face. With your blade planted fully in the water, your top hand will stay quite stationary, acting as a pivot point for the stroke, while you pull your lower hand in towards your hip. Now, before your paddle blade hits your kayak, you need to finish the stroke by slicing the blade out of the water towards the stern. This should happen when your blade is about six inches away from the side of your kayak. If you bring your blade in too close, it can accidentally get pinned against the side of your boat and throw you off balance.

T-Stroke Draw

1. The T-stroke is initiated the same way as the basic draw—with your head and upper body turned to face the active paddle blade.

2. Instead of slicing your paddle out of the water at the end of the draw, curl your wrists forward to turn the blade 90 degrees.

3. Slice your paddle back out to where it started.

4. Turn your wrists again and you're in position for another draw stroke.

When you get comfortable with the basic draw, you can try the T-stroke. The only difference between the T-stroke and the basic draw is that instead of slicing the blade out of the water towards the stern at the end of the stroke, you'll curl your wrists forward to turn the blade perpendicular to your boat and then slice it back out to where it started. Now you are set up to repeat the draw. This can be a very smooth and efficient way to move sideways.

If you find your boat turning as you take either a basic draw or T-stroke, it means that you're doing your draw too far forward or too far back. If your draw is too far forward, you'll pull your bow towards your paddle and your boat will turn. If your draw is too far back, you'll be pulling your stern towards your paddle.

Draw Strokes

Sculling Draw

An even more advanced technique for drawing your kayak sideways is called the sculling draw. Although it's more powerful than the other two draw strokes, it requires more paddle dexterity. It is a great stroke to learn once you're proficient with the other draw strokes. The sculling draw is set up in the same way as the T-stroke. Reaching out to the side of your hip, place your blade completely in the water with your head and upper body rotated aggressively to face it. Push your top hand across your boat to get your paddle as vertical as possible. Instead of pulling directly into your hip though, you'll use something we call a sculling motion. You now pull steadily on your paddle without having the blade draw closer to the side of your kayak. This removes the recovery phase that the other draw strokes require.

The key to sculling is keeping your paddle blade moving along a short path forward and backward about a foot or two out to the side of your kayak with a blade angle that opens your power face to the oncoming water and pulls your paddle away from your kayak. This unique blade angle is commonly referred to as a "climbing angle". Climbing angle means that the leading edge of your paddle blade is higher than the trailing edge. It uses the same motion that you unconsciously use when buttering bread. The leading edge has to stay higher than the trailing edge or else you're cutting into the bread. When you're learning the sculling draw, it can actually be a useful thing to visualize evenly spreading something thick like peanut butter on toast. To maintain a climbing angle on your blade while performing the sculling draw, you'll cock your wrists slightly back as you slice your blade forward. You then make a quick transition and curl your wrists slightly forward as you slice your blade backward. Keep in mind that the change in blade angle is subtle. If you open your power face too much, you'll be pushing your kayak forward and backward rather than drawing it sideways.

Using this sculling technique, you can apply steady drawing pressure with your paddle blade and move your boat sideways at a surprising speed. Don't forget that just like any other stroke; the power for your sculling draw comes from your torso rotation. This is why it's so important that you turn your body aggressively into the stroke. The forward and backward movement of your paddle can then be driven by your torso rotation, while your arms stay in a relatively fixed position.

1. Sculling involves moving your paddle blade along a short path alongside your kayak with the power face open to the oncoming water.

2. As you slice your blade forward, cock your wrists back slightly.

3. Notice the top hand acts much like a pivot point.

4. As you pull towards the stern, curl your wrists forward slightly.

5. With your hands held in relatively fixed positions, your torso rotation will provide much of the power for the stroke.

6. Throughout the sculling draw, the active blade remains one-and-a-half or two feet away from the side of your kayak.

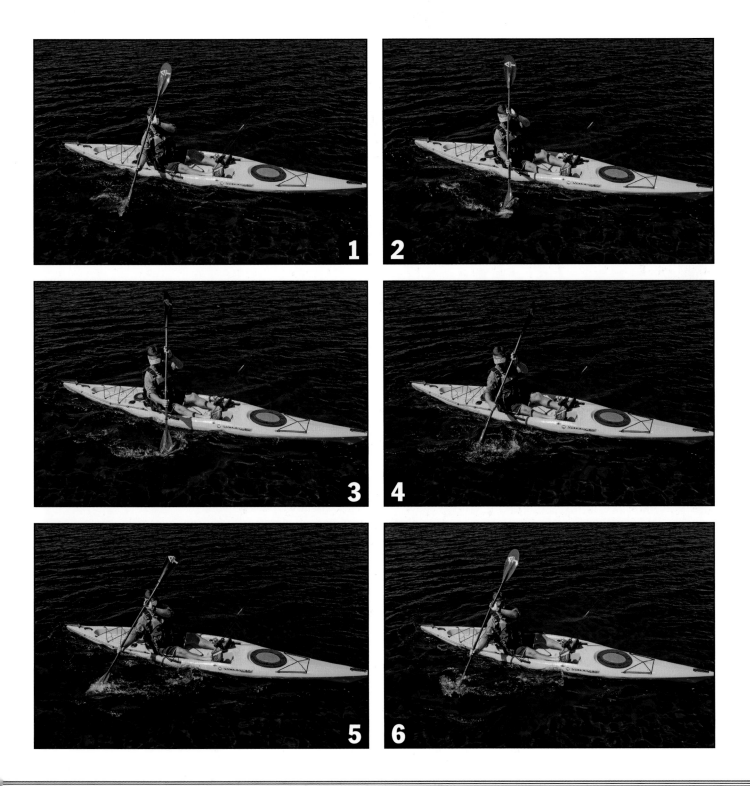

Your Kayak in Motion

I CAN STILL REMEMBER the first time that I set foot in a kayak. I was only 14 years old at the time and I was no stranger to the water. I had spent whole summers at the cottage, catching turtles and frogs from the canoe. Even with that experience, I remember being captivated with how effortlessly the kayak sliced its path through the water, and with how close I sat to the water. In hindsight, I'm not surprised that only two years later, my fascination blossomed into a full-blown kayaking addiction.

The way a kayak carves its path through the water is magical, but there's also a practical explanation for the way a kayak in motion performs. When you understand it, you'll be able to more accurately predict how your kayak will respond to your strokes, as well as to such things as wind and waves.

As the kayak slices through the water, water is hitting its front half. The water hitting the kayak is deflected and waves (or wake) are formed. The pressure of the water hitting the front of your kayak effectively holds it in place. This water pressure immediately disappears behind the widest point of the kayak (the center). In fact, from the center of the kayak all the way to the stern, where the kayak narrows, there is a low pressure zone, indicated by the lack of waves. The stern section of the kayak does not have nearly the same water pressure holding it in place, and so the stern can move much more freely from side-to-side. Understanding this, it should make sense when I say that any moving turns can be initiated most effectively with strokes at the stern of your kayak.

WIND

Weathercocking

You can now better appreciate the effect of a side (beam) wind on your kayak when you're traveling forward. Since your stern can move more freely from side to side than your bow, it will get pushed around more dramatically by wind. That's why every kayak will naturally turn into the wind (called weathercocking), unless a rudder or skeg is used to hold the stern in place. We'll look at how to use a rudder or skeg in the very next section about paddling in windy conditions.

All kayaks weathercock (turn into the wind) because the stern end of the kayak is more free to move side to side and will get blown downwind more quickly than the bow.

Paddling in Windy Conditions

THE SINGLE BIGGEST FACTOR affecting your ability to paddle (and to actually make reasonable progress) is wind. Wind can play havoc with how your kayak responds, can drum up large waves, and can even make moving forward impossible.

A knot is a unit of measure for speed. If you are traveling at a speed of 1 nautical mile per hour, you are said to be traveling at a speed of 1 knot.

The direction of the wind in relation to where you're traveling can have all sorts of different effects on your kayak. Obviously, a headwind will slow you right down. In fact, as a general rule, for every additional 5 knots of headwind, you can expect to be slowed down by 0.5 knots. A 20-knot headwind will slow you down by 2 full knots. Since an average paddler's speed is around 2.5 to 3 knots, your actual progress would be cut down to less than 1 knot! The only good thing about paddling into a headwind is that it usually means you're paddling directly into waves, which is the easiest way to deal with waves because you can see them coming and they don't tend to knock your boat off course.

Paddling with a tailwind is a different story altogether. The same general rule regarding the effects of wind applies—meaning that for every 5 knots of tailwind, you can expect to travel 0.5 knots faster. Throw some waves into the equation and you'll cruise along even faster than that as your boat catches mini-surfs on the faces of the waves. In fact, the right waves will let you surf your way downwind without taking any strokes at all. By the same token, wind waves will also make traveling downwind more challenging because you can't easily see them coming. Over time and with experience you'll develop a general paddling awareness which will let you confidently paddle in these conditions. Until then, you can expect to feel a little uneasy with your back to the wind and waves. In fact, some people will even get seasick when paddling with their backs to the waves as their boat unpredictably pitches forward and back.

The trickiest wind conditions for paddling are beam (side) winds. Not only will you usually have to deal with waves coming at you from the side, but your kayak will want to turn into the wind, or weathercock. This where a rudder or skeg will come in really handy, and we're about to look at how they are used. If you don't have a rudder or skeg, you can expect to have to paddle harder on the upwind side of your kayak to

 **Tip** A nautical mile is a unit of measurement used by all nations for air and sea travel. It's equal to 1.151 standard miles, or one minute of latitude at the earth's equator. What is a minute of latitude? Well, if you were to cut the Earth in half at the equator, the flat surface would be a circle. Now divide that circle into 360 degrees. Then further divide one of those degrees into 60 equal segments, which are called minutes. The distance of the arc for one minute of our Earth is equal to 1 nautical mile.

Tip Most areas have somewhat predictable winds, although you can never be certain what the wind is going to do. If you're new to an area, take the time to learn the common wind patterns and choose your trips accordingly. For example, you might find that in the area you intend to fish, the wind always seems to pick up around midday, and then dies down in the evening. This probably means that a morning fish is your best choice.

compensate for the weathercocking of your boat. Over a long distance, this can make travel exhausting, but if the wind is strong enough, you'll find this to be a real pain even over a short distance.

The trickiest wind conditions to deal with are when the wind and waves are coming from an angle behind and to the side of your kayak. In this case, instead of paddling directly to your end destination, you might be better off paddling directly downwind and then turning 90 degrees to paddle to your end destination perpendicular to the wind. This means traveling further, but the paddling will be much easier.

Using Rudders or Skegs

As you now know, the main purpose of rudders and skegs is to keep a kayak going straight when paddling in wind. When moving forward with a side wind, a kayak will naturally turn into the wind, or weathercock. A rudder or skeg can counteract this effect by holding the stern in place.

Because rudders swivel side-to-side (unlike skegs), they are much more powerful for controlling a kayak and also much more popular than skegs for kayak fishing. Rudders flip down from their stored position on top of the deck using haul lines that are found alongside the cockpit. Rudders are controlled from the cockpit using your foot pedals. By pushing forward on your right foot pedal, you'll cause your

boat to turn to the right; push on the left and you'll turn to the left. Besides helping you to keep your boat on course when paddling in wind or current, and helping to turn your kayak in tight places, one of the great advantages to having a rudder is that it allows you to control the angle of your kayak with your feet during a downwind drift. This leaves your hands free to do what you're there for... to catch fish!

Skegs are stored in a skeg box embedded in the stern of the kayak; they are deployed by use of a slider found alongside the cockpit. Because skegs don't swivel side to side, their control comes from the depth at which they are set. The more your kayak wants to weathercock, the deeper you'll set the skeg. Since skegs are only really useful for tracking over long distances, you generally don't find them on fishing kayaks.

> **Tip**
When trolling, the drag of your lure through the water will cause your kayak to turn slightly to the side that you're trolling. The bigger the lure, the more impact it will have in this way. You can use this to help counter weathercocking by trolling off the downwind side of your kayak.

Reentering Your Kayak from the Water

ALTHOUGH KAYAKS are very stable, it's common sense to be prepared for the unlikely situation that requires you to reenter your kayak from the water. One of the huge advantages of sit-on-top kayaks is that they are so easy to get back into from the water. Divers have used these types of boats for years for the simple reason that they can easily hop into the water and make a dive from them. When the dive is over they can throw their tank and gear back on top and climb aboard. Sit-inside kayaks simply don't provide this flexibility—but with a little practice and some help from a friend, you can learn to quickly and reliably reenter a sit-inside. The problem remaining is that since sit-insides aren't self-bailing, you'll have a lot of water to pump out of your kayak once you're back in the seat.

The most important thing in having the confidence to reenter either style of kayak is practice, practice, practice! You can't just do it once and think you've got it figured out. Start off on flat, calm water and get your technique down. Once you get comfortable with your abilities, move to some rougher water and try again, because there's a good chance that you'll be in rough conditions when you flip. If you live near the coast, the surf is a great place to test yourself with sit-inside kayaks; just make sure to wear your PFD and have at least one buddy with you while practicing.

Reentering a Sit-On-Top

If you fish from a sit-on-top kayak for long, there's a reasonable chance that you'll find yourself taking an unscheduled swim and needing to get back on top of your kayak from the water. Hopefully your kayak didn't actually flip over, and if it did, any equipment that wasn't stored inside was tied down. If it did flip upside-down, you can right your boat by approaching it from the side and scrambling over the hull to grab the far edge. In this position, you will have the leverage necessary to right the kayak by pulling it towards you. Pushing up on the near side is much more difficult. When practicing, try both methods to get a better understanding of what we're talking about.

Once the kayak is right-side-up, getting back in is a fairly simple process, but it does require a small amount of explosive power. Start by positioning yourself alongside the kayak, by the seat. You can keep your paddle in one hand, slide it under your deck lines so that it doesn't get away from you, or give it to your paddling buddy. With a firm grip on the kayak, let your legs float to the surface behind you. You'll then give a powerful kick with your legs and push with your arms to haul your chest up onto the kayak. Once you're up on the boat, twist your body around and settle into the seat. You can then swing your legs back onto the boat. The whole process may not look pretty, but it works!

1–3: To get back into a sit-on-top, approach the kayak from the side and get your feet on the surface of the water behind you. Then, with a kick of the legs and a push up with the arms, draw your body on top of the kayak, keeping your weight low.

4–6: With the hard part accomplished, you can spin and drop your butt into the seat, and then pull your legs in.

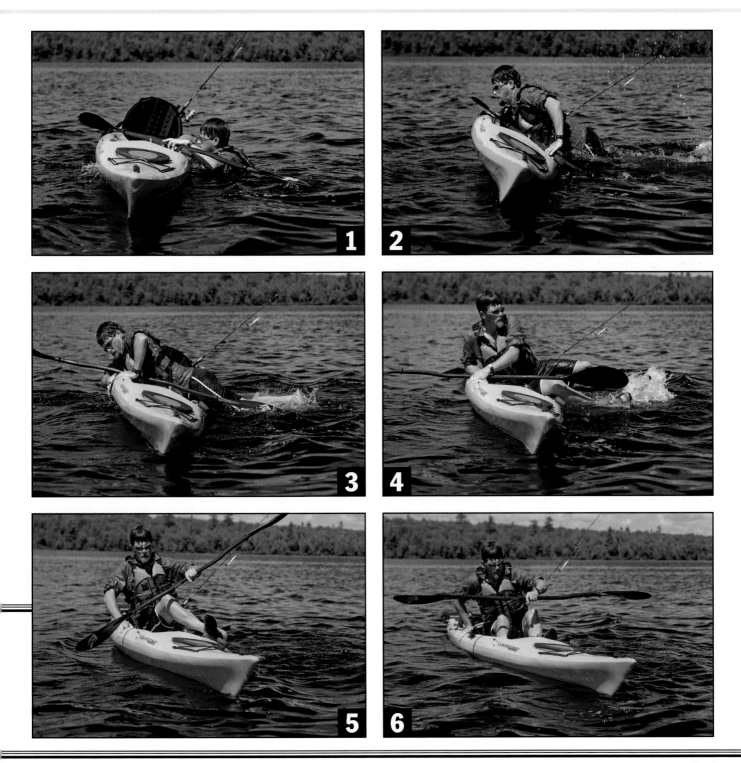

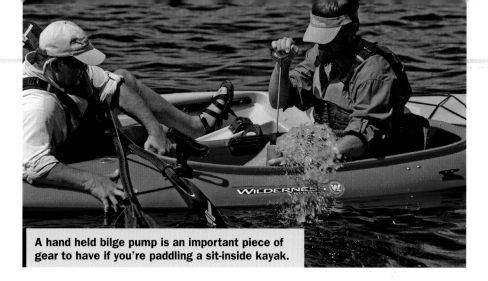

A hand held bilge pump is an important piece of gear to have if you're paddling a sit-inside kayak.

1. The swimmer will use the same reentry technique for a sit-inside as was just demonstrated for the sit-on-top, except he'll need the help of a friend to support his kayak.

2. The rescuer gets a firm grip on the bow and leans his weight onto the empty boat to stabilize it while the swimmer reenters.

3. Once the swimmer has pulled himself on top of the kayak, he'll spin and drop his butt into the seat.

4. The rescuer needs to maintain his support of the swimmer's kayak throughout the reentry.

Reentering a Sit-Inside

A sit-inside kayak presents a different set of problems. It holds water and will be unstable while you climb on top of it, right up until the point when you are settled back into the cockpit. For these reasons, reentering a sit-inside kayak is much easier with the help of another paddler.

If you've found yourself swimming from a sit-inside, chances are very good that your boat is upside-down. The first order of business is to flip your boat upright. When your boat is upside-down, air gets trapped inside. The trapped air keeps water from flooding the interior. This means that the quicker you can flip the boat upright, the less water will get scooped inside. Although you can flip the kayak upright yourself from the water, it is easier if your paddling buddy helps by lifting an end as you roll the kayak. With the kayak upright, your paddling partner can then stabilize the kayak as you get back in. A partner can actually provide an incredible amount of stability, although it requires a lot of commitment on his or her part. To assist, your partner positions his or her kayak parallel to yours and gets a good grip on the empty kayak with both hands, then leans his/her whole body over onto it. As long as he has a good grip on the kayak, there's virtually no chance of his flipping himself, as the two "rafted" kayaks will be extremely stable. You can then use virtually the same reentry technique as the one we just outlined for getting back into the sit-on-top kayak. You need to remember that your center of gravity will be high and this will make your kayak unstable until you've got your butt back in the seat.

Of course, once you're back inside, you'll have a fair amount of water in the boat to deal with. This is where a bilge pump comes in handy. Be sure to keep your pump stored in such a manner that it is easily accessed, but also secure enough that it doesn't float away during the capsizing. Although a bilge pump is a great piece of safety gear for any sit-inside kayak, it's a good idea to make a practice of staying close enough to shore so that you can easily head to dry land and empty your boat there.

CHAPTER 5

fishing from a kayak

NOW WE'VE GOTTEN you through the selection of your kayak and gear, you've learned how to outfit your boat, and you've become an outstanding paddler. You are starting to walk the walk and talk the talk. So what's next? Like our buddy Dean Thomas always says, "You sure talk like you know what you're doing, but sooner or later you're gonna have to catch a fish." He's right. That's why you got into this whole thing in the first place. You wanted to catch fish from a kayak. We can all say it isn't about catching fish, it's about the exercise or it's about the pure pleasure of getting outdoors. While those things are great and it sounds cool to say, we all really know…it's about the fish.

So the fish has finally cooperated and you find yourself at one end of a tug-of-war with a finned adversary. What do you do now? You would be surprised how many people who have just started kayak fishing fail to plan for this part of the adventure. We've had the front row seats for some pretty funny scenes when the two parties meet for the first time. Rods get broken, people drop their nets in the water, and on one occasion, a 5-pound redfish flipped a 200-pound grown man off his kayak. That fella looked pretty silly sitting in the water in the mud right next to his trusty steed. Luckily it only injured his pride. In deeper water it could have been serious.

The way to avoid this dilemma is by being prepared and having a plan. The biggest part of the plan is having a good idea what type and size of fish you are targeting. It doesn't hurt to know what other non-targeted fish might be encountered in the area. For instance, take fishing in the surf zone just outside the breakers for speckled trout. These fish generally run from 3 to 5 pounds with an occasional larger fish, but anything over 10 pounds is extremely rare. You can rig up for this easily enough with standard bay gear. A medium/light action rod and reel, 12-pound line, and a variety of lures will do the trick. To land one of these fish is a simple matter of reaching out and grabbing it with a firm grip across the back, or by netting it. There are no problems with this plan, except that trout aren't the only possibility out there. What happens when a 20-pound king mackerel attacks your lure? It isn't normal, but it isn't all that unheard of, either. Kings are extremely fast predators with razor-sharp teeth. The possibilities for disaster large or small abound in this situation for the unprepared angler.

Big fish are much stronger than you think and are quite capable of inflicting serious injury if improperly handled. This is not meant to discourage anyone from paddling after the biggest, meanest fish to ever swim: just don't try it the first time you go out. Get comfortable with your equipment and hone your abilities on smaller species, while working your way up to the big leagues. There are people new to kayaking who are dead set on fishing the surf zone and ocean passes for mature redfish. These brutes can easily top 40 pounds and they live in an environment that can be downright dangerous, even for experienced kayakers. Beginners, and even some people with years of experience, have no business out there pursuing fish like this. We wrote this segment to give you a foundation to work from and to give you some things to consider before you inevitably become attached to a fish that is bigger than you planned.

Scott plays a big redfish in the flats of Texas.

Fighting Fish from a Kayak

Hooking and fighting a fish is the rush that brings us back time and again. No matter how many fish you've caught, doing it from a kayak is a whole new experience. If you hook a big enough fish, you'll suddenly find yourself being pulled across the water. It is an odd feeling the first few times a fish grabs a hold of your lure and spins your yak around like a weather vane. The coolest trip you'll ever have in kayak fishing is when a truly big fish decides to head for the horizon with you in tow.

While targeting smaller panfish and such, getting towed around isn't a concern. For this type of fishing, you may or may not decide you need to anchor yourself. The wind may be the biggest factor in deciding whether you do or not, although if you're in shallow water, you might just sit side-saddle with your feet on the bottom to hold your position. It doesn't get much easier than this.

With somewhat larger fish inshore or in lakes, it may become necessary to plan for being towed or at the very least spun around. This is fine out in

open water on a calm day. Kick back and enjoy the ride. However, if you're in a situation where being towed could be unsafe or cause you to lose the fish due to some line-entangling structure, then you need to do something. In shallow water, it is fairly simple to stop yourself if you're in a sit-on-top. Simply swing your legs over the side and plant your feet firmly on the bottom. Problem solved. Another tactic to use in shallow water with a sand or mud bottom is to deploy a stake-out pole that's tethered to your kayak. Once the fish is on, you grab the stake-out pole and stick it into the bottom. You can also place the pole through one of your scupper holes instead of having it tethered like an anchor. This is very quick, simple, and effective.

Deeper inshore water requires a little more forethought. You should be ready to deploy your anchor if it's not already deployed. This sounds easy enough until you try it while being pulled across the water with your drag screaming. At that moment, you'll want to have your anchor handy and ready to go. Now is not the time to retrieve the anchor from your tank well, clip it to your kayak, and hope the rope isn't tangled.

There is another very quick and effective method for dealing with these situations. Like most good ideas, this one was born from necessity while

Howard McKim swings his legs over the sides of the kayak to help stabilize himself while pulling a big halibut up.

fishing in Florida for snook, way back in the mangroves for the first time. Snook are ambush feeders and they love to hang close to the edges of the trees. Their immediate response to feeling the sting of a hook is to turn and run straight into a tangle of mangrove roots. These fish were simply yanking our kayaks right into the trees. We were getting schooled and the tally of lost lures was mounting. The problem was that the water was too deep to touch bottom, and it was necessary to remain mobile while working down the shoreline. Anchoring would have been ineffective.

The solution was to set the anchor up with a length of rope just long enough to hit bottom and with enough scope to allow the anchor to grab. The anchor rope is then clipped onto a cleat or pad eye and the shank of the anchor is placed in a flush-mount rod holder. The location of the anchor depends on which hand you crank your reel with. If you use your left hand, place the anchor in a rod holder just behind and to the left of your seat. You can then ease along, casting perpendicular to the shoreline trees. Once a fish is hooked, hold the rod with one hand and toss out the anchor with the other. The anchor grabs the bottom and with a tight drag you've got a fighting chance at keeping the fish out of whatever line-cutting structure is around.

Dean Thomas puts pressure on a fish heading to the stern so that he can pivot the kayak and avoid his other fishing rods.

The opposite of that situation is when you are fishing at anchor and hook up with a very large fish in open water. It is often advantageous to let a big strong fish tow you around a bit. You are in effect using your kayak as drag to wear the fish down. The problem is that you can't very well retrieve and stow your anchor while doing battle. The solution here is to attach the anchor to your kayak using a quick release clip and have a brightly colored float rigged on the rope near the clip. Once a fish is on the line, release the anchor clip and fight your fish. When the fight is over, locate the float and paddle back to it. Then you can either retrieve the anchor, or reattach it to your kayak and resume fishing in the same spot.

Another twist on using your kayak as drag to tire out a fish is to deploy a drift anchor during the fight. This will produce a serious amount of drag, but it also increases the odds that the fish could foul in the trailing line or the drift anchor. We have a friend in Florida who often uses this technique for landing ridiculously large tarpon from his kayak.

Inevitably, a fish will run underneath your kayak. You need to quickly assess the situation and determine whether or not you can turn the fish. Hopefully you'll be able to impose your will and bring it back out from under the boat. Should you realize that this won't work, you'd better be ready to react quickly. The big fellow we mentioned earlier found himself in this position and made the momentary mistake of leaning over

Ken Whiting uses one arm on his paddle to control his kayak while fighting a nice smallmouth bass on the Ottawa River.

the side of the kayak to see where the fish was going. He was out of the kayak and sitting in the mud before he knew what happened. A large fish can easily flip you over, or break a rod against the side of the kayak. The best thing to do is extend your rod tip towards the front of the kayak, clear the line around the bow, and resume the fight. This might not work if the fish went under the kayak and angled towards the stern. The best way to handle that situation is to extend the rod tip at an angle out and back towards the stern while bearing down and putting as much pressure as you dare on the fish. The goal here is to pivot the kayak. It probably won't work too well if you have an anchor out.

Something else to practice is using one arm to paddle. It is a very handy skill to have in your arsenal. This usually comes into play in moving water, or when a fish is towing the kayak towards an obstacle. Be aware of your surroundings and be prepared to use the paddle to maneuver. I like to position the paddle with the center near my elbow and the shaft along the outside of my forearm.

With a firm grip, I can now brace the shaft of the paddle against my forearm and reposition the kayak as needed.

The secret to success with any of these methods is in knowing exactly what the plan is before you ever hook the fish. You must be familiar with your equipment and have the ability to use it without having to take your mind off the fight. Battling a big, strong fish from a kayak is challenging enough when you've got it all together—imagine what it would be like if you were completely unprepared for the experience.

Landing Fish in a Kayak

As stated previously, catching small fish from a kayak doesn't require much forethought or planning. Quite often it is just a matter of hoisting them into the cockpit while they're still hooked. Large fish are a completely different story, as are toothy critters. Again, knowing your quarry and being prepared for the possibility of incidental catches will help. Common sense will determine whether you'll be using your hand, a net, a lip-gripping tool, or possibly a gaff.

For instance, barracuda are a real possibility on the flats in Florida, even though the target is bonefish. There's a huge difference in safely landing these two fish. A bonefish is easily picked up with a hand placed under its belly while a barracuda's vicious teeth and generally bad attitude demand respect and a cautious approach.

A few words about conservation seem appropriate at this point. If you intend to release the fish, it is best to use a lip-gripping tool or your hand. Nets are tough on a fish's protective slime coating—and while the fish might appear to be fine when it's released, it could suffer from skin infections later on. A lip-gripping tool is very effective for gaining control of a fish and minimizes the amount of handling required to unhook and release it. Just remember that the classic fish photo method of hanging a large fish vertically by its lips can cause injury to the jaw hinge and internal organs. If you'd like to get a picture of your catch before releasing it, try holding it horizontally with one hand supporting the belly. Should you choose to use your hand, always wet it prior to grabbing the fish to lessen the effects on its slime coating.

The final moments of fighting a fish are critical to safely landing it. The majority of fish lost happen within a few feet of the angler. A combination of factors conspire to cause this last-second escape. Excitement overtakes reasoning and good judgment. The trophy seems to be a sure thing and the angler prematurely makes a grab, causing the fish to surge away. At this point, physics takes over. There is less line to act as a shock absorber and the rod is bent to the point that it has also lost its shock-absorbing qualities. Without the extra

A lip gripping tool, like Boga grips, are one of the handiest tools for landing fish from a kayak. They help protect both you and the fish.

By bending the elbow and bringing the reel into the body when the fish is in close, your arm can provide some of the shock absorbing qualities that your rod and line can no longer deliver.

give in the rod, the pressure on the hook increases and it pulls free—or the line breaks. To provide a little insurance, many experienced anglers will back off on the drag just a bit as the fish gets closer. Another thing you'll see great anglers do is sharply bend at the elbow, bringing the reel up close to the body. If the fish makes a sudden surge they can then extend the arm, allowing for a bit of give to the fish. The angler who can remain calm and steady will be the one who consistently lands the trophy fish.

When in shallow water, many anglers choose to exit their kayak and bring the fish to hand while standing in the water. This is a great tactic if you are certain of the depth of water and the composition of the bottom. Stepping out into deep water or onto a soft bottom will not win you any style points with your fishing buddies, but the good news is, you'll be the center of attention back at fish camp during the storytelling hour. So, if you are the least bit uncertain of

 **Tip** As a general rule, when landing a fish, leave a good rod's length of line out so that you can bring the fish in close to the side of the kayak. This also gives you enough line to lay down your rod in between your legs after getting hold of the fish, so that you have two hands free for releasing it.

either, you're much better off staying put in your boat.

The key to landing large fish whether wading, in a boat, or in a kayak is to play the fish until it is properly tired to the point when it is safe to handle. The last thing you want in the kayak is an out-of-control fish. In fact, very large fish that you intend to release are best left in the water alongside the kayak. Keep in mind that maintaining your weight over the centerline of the kayak will help you remain upright. Leaning over to hoist a big fish into the cockpit could lead to an unexpected swim. You must realize that the fish's weight does not have any impact on your balance while it is in the water. As you lift that fish from the water the amount of off-center weight is increasing and you need to compensate by placing an equal amount of your weight towards the opposite side of the kayak. Know the limit of stability on your particular kayak and don't exceed it. It sounds so simple, but in the heat of the moment the excitement can cause a lapse in judgment.

Do yourself a favor and get as much information as possible about the fish you may encounter, especially in saltwater. Some, like barracuda or king mackerel, have obviously dangerous dentures, while others conceal their defenses. A snook can safely be grabbed by the lower lip in the classic bass-fishing manner. However, they have a

Jim Sammons leaves a rod-length of line out and controls the rod with his right hand just above the reel to bring a lingcod alongside his kayak and in position for his lip gripper.

razor-sharp gill plate that has cut many an unsuspecting angler. Spotted sea trout look innocent enough, but they've got a set of needle-sharp teeth towards the front of the mouth that will cause a serious puncture wound should you attempt to grab by the lip. Know your quarry and you'll be better prepared to deal with the chore of landing.

Should you decide to keep a few fish for dinner, you'll need to find a way to store them. A stringer is simple and generally effective. You can also carry along a soft-sided ice chest or one of the insulated bags designed for bringing your cold foods home from the grocery store. Another option is to get one of the insulated kayak fish bags that are specifically designed to be used by kayakers. These triangular-shaped, soft-side coolers can be strapped to the front deck or placed in the rear tank well and will hold a surprising amount of ice and fish.

Jim uses two hands to control a feisty lingcod.

Big Game Kayak Fishing

By Jim Sammons

In recent years, kayak fishing has seen growth unlike any other part of either fishing or paddlesports. Now it seems that if there is water with fish to target you will find kayak anglers. While many people are content to catch the smaller, inshore varieties of fish (not that there is anything wrong with that!) there is a growing desire to target the bigger game fish that haunt the coast. For these anglers, the sensation of getting dragged around the sea has become an addiction for which they must get another fix.

I can tell you from personal experience that catching a 200-pound thresher shark or a 180-pound striped marlin from a 15-foot, 60-pound kayak is something that gets your heart pumping and your adrenalin flowing like nothing else. One thing that holds true for any big catch is the adrenalin factor that comes from bringing a fish to color that can actually hurt you—and I mean not just sore-muscles-hurt, but physical-damage-hurt. The experience of a thresher shark greyhounding across the water towards you, a marlin slashing his bill out of the water as you try to land it, or a tarpon leaping out of the water mere feet way, will cause even the heartiest of us to wonder if this is the smartest thing to be doing. But for some reason, we'll keep doing it every chance we get.

Targeting big game from the kayak is not to be taken lightly; the inexperienced can quickly find that they have taken on more than they bargained for. Landing a fish that would take 15 minutes on 100-

Jim pulls hard on a big halibut in Alaska.

pound-test line from a cruiser could take well over an hour from a kayak—during which time you could get dragged for many miles. In fact, I've had fights over three hours long with marlin that have dragged me over five miles straight out to sea, at speeds that would amaze any onlooker. My good friend Howard McKim caught a 183-pound halibut up in Alaska, and from the moment he hooked it until he was back home on the beach, almost eight hours had gone by.

If you've decided that you want to target big game from a kayak, here's my advice. First off, make sure you do your research on the characteristics of the fish you want to target, so that you know what to expect once you've got a fish on. There is a lot of great information available on the web, but the best thing to do in the early stages is to hire a guide, or at the very least go out with someone with lots of experience with the fish. They will not only help you avoid situations that may get you in trouble, but also help put you on the fish.

1. Matt Moyer catches a 130-pound striped marlin.

2. The marlin jumps a little too close for comfort.

3. Matt keeps the pressure on to tire the marlin enough to handle.

4. Landing a fish of this size is much safer with two people.

5. Matt Moyer and Jim Sammons celebrate.

6. To revive the marlin, Jim holds on while getting towed by the powerboat.

Big Game Gear

When selecting your kayak for targeting big fish, look for one in which you feel stable and comfortable. I often use one of the larger singles or a tandem when targeting thresher sharks, so that I have a nice, stable, landing platform. For other types of fishing, I'll usually opt for a narrow and faster kayak, so I can travel more efficiently.

The way I rig my kayak for big game is pretty much the same as I rig it for all other types of fishing. I like to keep everything within easy reach, but out of the way for when I'm fighting and landing a fish. For the most part, this means keeping the front deck clear of anything but essentials like my fish finder. This not only eliminates obstacles for landing the fish but also keeps my view clear for scanning the horizon for signs of fish.

If I'm trolling live bait, I prefer to use a rocket-launcher style of rod holder, placed behind me. This keeps the reel up out of the water and again keeps my vision clear in front. All told, I have 13 rod holders on my kayak which all get used at different times for different fishing styles and situations. You need to rig your kayak up so that you feel comfortable. Just keep the idea that you want your gear "accessible but out of the way" and you will be much better off.

As far as your fishing equipment goes, using fresh line and leader with a reel that has a smooth drag and strong side plates can make the difference between landing and losing the fish of a lifetime. The reels don't have to be big. The fact that your kayak acts as drag opens up a lot of possibilities for fishing big game from a kayak with light tackle. I personally have landed a 67-pound shark with 6-pound-test line. In fact, I caught my first marlin while fishing for yellowtail off La Jolla with only 20-pound-test on my Shimano Charter Special. Lucky for me, it was brand new line! My buddy Matt landed a marlin at the same time on a small Shimano Trinidad 12, with only 30-pound-test.

The fight lasted two-and-a-half hours and covered eight miles.

For line, I like to use 20- to 40-pound-test mono or 55-pound-test Spectra if I'm fishing with a smaller reel. For billfish or sharks I'll then use a long (6- to 12-foot) mono or fluorocarbon leader of 80- to 100-pound-test.

You also need a rod long enough to reach around the bow of your kayak (7-foot is a good length), because you can expect big fish to run back and forth under your kayak. A 6-foot rod will give you a bit more leverage on those real big fish, but I would avoid going any shorter.

Greg Bowdish puts his weight into a fight with a tarpon.

Fighting Big Fish

When it comes to fighting a big fish from a kayak, if you are fishing with live bait, you will need to keep the reel out of gear with the clicker on, so when a fish hits, it can run with the bait and not rip the rod holder off the boat or send you swimming. So having a reel with a strong clicker is imperative, particularly if fishing larger baits like mackerel or mullet. When trolling with artificials I prefer not to use a rod holder; I simply tuck the rod under my leg and arm. This allows me to set the hook right away by simply taking a few hard forward strokes of my paddle, without putting undue pressure on the kayak itself. It can be a bear to remove the rod from a rod holder if it is loaded up with the weight of even a small fish, let alone a big muskie or tarpon.

Once you get that big one on the line, this is where the fun starts: you can get that coveted sleigh ride, which sometimes lasts for miles. This is where knowing your prey really comes into play. Does the fish go deep or run out? Is it a jumper, or is it known to run to structures? All these things will impact your strategy for fighting the fish. If you have a fish that tends to run out on the surface, you can fish a much tighter drag than you may be accustomed to when fishing from shore or a boat, because the fish will

be pulling your kayak in tow. Your kayak actually acts as a form of drag itself, so you are not really pulling as hard on the fish as you might think. Of course, this theory doesn't apply to fish that go deep. The bottom line is that if a big fish runs out on you, you really don't need to give them much line. Let them pull your boat. This may help you land that fish that likes to run into structure.

For more erratic fish, such as tuna (which seem to be going right and left at the same time) you might want to use a little lighter drag pressure during the early fight stages, in order to keep the fish from pulling you off of your yak. A lever-drag reel is a great way to go with these bigger fish, because it is much easier to quickly change your drag pressure without losing your optimal setting.

Sometimes you'll want to put even more pressure on a big fish than the drag of your kayak alone can supply, and a simple way to do this is to drop your feet into the water over the sides. Not only does this increase the drag, but it gives you better leverage and more balance. You can also spin your kayak sideways and sit side saddle to force the fish to pull the entire kayak sideways through the water, or, if you're fishing with a friend (which I highly recommend when big game kayak fishing) you can have them hold onto your kayak so that the fish needs to pull the weight of both of you. We actually had a marlin drag four kayakers and a swimmer through the water at one time.

Some people will deploy a drift chute to put more pressure on a fish. I don't like this technique because there's a very real chance of losing the fish if your line gets wrapped up in the chute.

Just remember that when using any of these methods, you are not only putting more pressure on the fish, but more pressure on you. Sometimes it is better to just sit back and enjoy the ride, let the fish tire itself out while taking you on a tour of the local waters. You will have more energy left when you need it—during the end game.

Jim gets towed by a tarpon in the shark-infested and dangerous waters of Boca Grande in Southwest Florida. Jim had two support/safety boats on hand at the time.

The End Game

Although tiring, the fight is the easy part of big game kayak fishing. Landing a fish (what we call the "end game") is where things can get really tricky and potentially very dangerous. The dangers associated with landing a fish with a 3-foot-long spear on its face, a 6-foot tail, or a mouth full of large, razor-sharp teeth, are fairly obvious and definitely shouldn't be taken lightly. Many things can go wrong, and the situation can get very serious very quickly if you're not prepared for dealing with it.

Before you even get out on the water, you should think through the whole fight so that you'll have the tools on hand that you'll need. Do you have the proper landing tools—a gaff, landing net, tail rope, game clip, or gloves? There are often specific regulations on which landing tools can be used in different regions for certain species. For the safety of the fish, some can't even be lifted from the water. It's also very important that you have (and always wear): a PFD in case you end up swimming; a VHF radio so you can call for help; and a cut-away tool attached to your PFD, in case you hook onto something that you're not prepared to land.

One of the best ways to protect yourself when landing a big fish is to take your time. The last thing you want is a green fish slashing or

Greg gets ready to land a tired and therefore safe-to-handle tarpon.

jumping around your kayak. For this very reason, when I have clients hook billfish, I always tell them to fight the fish away from the boat. When you first hook up, let that fish take all the line it wants, so you are fighting the fish from a safe distance. Some of the most dangerous fights come from smaller or juvenile big game fish, as they tend to turn toward your kayak quickly, and the next thing you know they are jumping towards you. Be patient and you'll win the battle! Most fish you will encounter are easy to manage solo, but as you get into bigger fish, having a buddy there will be a huge asset in not only landing fish, but also in reviving fish that you intend to release. When I target shark or billfish, I always fish with a friend and have a support boat ready. These fish will fight you until the end and it can be difficult to give them a good, healthy release when fishing alone. A support boat, besides being a great safety feature, can also help you with the catch and release by towing you while you hold the fish's bill, which forces fresh water through its gills until it's ready to swim off on its own.

Although you can land pretty much any fish from a kayak if you have the patience and equipment, there are some fish that it simply makes sense to avoid.

One of Jim's clients catches a record roosterfish in Baja.

Kayak Fishing Techniques

The fun-to-danger ratio simply isn't in your favor when you have something like a mako shark on the line. In fact, this is one of the reasons I use mono leaders when fishing for sharks. The nasty mako teeth are more likely to bite through it for a nice, easy release.

Probably the most important thing you can bring when fishing for big game is your common sense. It is easy to get caught up in the moment when fighting or landing a big fish, but you should never lose sight of the very real dangers involved. Don't hesitate to ask for help from your friends or guide if you think you need it, and don't take any chances just so you can get that glory shot. There are often times when it is best to just cut the line next to the mouth and let a fish go.

As I stand on my soapbox, let me also take this opportunity to implore you to practice catch, photo, and release with big game fish. When it comes to the apex predators, there simply are not enough of them around to kill on a regular basis, and so I highly recommend releasing all of them. And although I have no issue with keeping other fish for food (and I do so on a regular basis), try to keep only what you will eat that day and let the rest go. I look at it this way: why have frozen fish when you can have fresh fish? Even better, if there is no fish in the freezer, you have a great excuse to go fishing again!

Now that you're a bit more prepared for getting a fish on line, it is time to discuss some of the best methods for catching those fish. Assuming that you already have a basic idea of how to fish, it is just a matter of adapting your fishing style to the kayak. Fishing methods vary greatly throughout the country, depending on the locale, conditions, and the species being sought. It would be quite presumptuous, not to mention unbelievable, for us to pretend that we could cover every situation encountered by anglers everywhere. Just thumbing through the national fishing supply catalogues can leave you scratching your head, trying to figure out what some of these contraptions are used for. Even with all the varied methods and species, there aren't too many fishing situations that can't be handled from a kayak.

This segment covers the basic fishing techniques that can be adapted to fit more area-specific needs. For more regional fishing information, check out the special segments in the Saltwater Kayak Fishing and the Freshwater Kayak Fishing chapters.

Trolling

Trolling from a powerboat is a very effective way of catching fish. The same is true from a kayak. Some people choose to drift with the current or wind while dragging a lure or bait. Others choose to propel themselves at a steady pace with their paddle. Both styles have one thing in common: the most successful anglers don't simply drift along or paddle without purpose—they will concentrate their efforts by passing over or near some sort of structure. This is a much higher-percentage method than aimlessly covering water. The type of structure targeted depends on the type of fish you are seeking. As stated earlier, it is assumed that you have a basic understanding of the fish you want to target in your area. Use that knowledge and the kayak to your advantage.

Perhaps one of the most exciting methods of kayak trolling is to target actively feeding schools of fish on the surface. Predators blitzing baitfish often draw gulls or other birds to the fray. Watch for a tight group of birds hovering and diving into the water. This is your flashing neon sign. Once you figure out which way the school is headed, you can set yourself up to intercept them. Try to pass in front of the school, and time it so that your trailing lure passes through the leading edge of the school. The most aggressively feeding fish will usually be at the front of the pack. This is where the kayak really shines. A kayaker can pass much closer to the activity than a powerboat without spooking the fish. On a recent trip, we made numerous passes straight through the middle of the melee. The fish were moving so fast that it was nearly impossible not to do so, but it didn't seem to have any effect on the feeding frenzy. We probably couldn't have gotten away with running a powerboat through them.

Brendan Mark and Joel McBride troll along a weedline on Grand Lac Dumoine in Quebec, Canada.

Your biggest decision when setting up to troll is where to place your rod. Of course, this is a matter of preference. Many anglers (myself included) like to use flush-mount or mounted rod holders just behind the seat because it keeps the rod and line out of their paddles' way and keeps the front deck clear when fighting a fish. Other anglers like to use rod holders up front, which point the rod directly out to the side of the kayak. The advantage of doing this is that you can easily monitor the rod's action while you paddle. Some anglers will even troll with their rod held between their legs instead of in a rod holder. This lets you monitor the action closely, but it can make it a little more awkward to paddle.

Something to keep in mind while you're trolling is the effect of wind and waves on your kayak. Your kayak can get pushed around a great deal by both, which means that you often need to pay extra attention to your trolling speed to ensure you're getting the right action from your lure. For example, you may be able to troll at a very leisurely pace when paddling with the wind at your back, but if you're facing the wind, you may need to paddle considerably harder to maintain the lure's speed through the water. The same goes for paddling in wavy conditions. When paddling in the same direction as the waves, your boat will likely surge forward as it momentarily catches a surf on the wave.

When you're paddling against waves, your kayak may stall out momentarily as a wave passes underneath you; you may want to accelerate immediately before the wave hits you.

Some kayak anglers prefer trolling with two or more rigs, but we feel this invites catastrophe, and it's even illegal in some areas. With actively feeding fish, the chances of hooking more than one fish are fairly high, and this is not the most desirable situation when you're alone in a small craft. Dealing with one bent rod while stowing the paddle and trying to keep everything under control is hard enough. Multiply the number of hooked fish and you'll quickly learn the meaning of chaos.

For this type of fishing it is essential to have a good quality rod holder that is securely attached to the kayak. A large fish hitting a lure full force will surely test your equipment. Riveted rod holders could be ripped loose in these situations. Depending on the type of fish you're targeting, it might make sense to attach the rod holders to your kayak with bolts, washers, and nuts—and as an added precaution, you can even use a rod leash. As stated above, this is an exciting type of fishing. Many things can happen all at once and it only takes a minimal lapse in concentration to lose a rod while trying to secure your paddle and retrieve your rig from the holder.

Drift Fishing

Drift fishing is our common method for covering water. Fishing the coast often means dealing with the wind, so you may as well work with it instead of trying to fight it. The term "drift fishing" sounds as though you are aimlessly floating with wind or current, but when done correctly, it is a high-percentage method of searching for fish. This is where a rudder can be a real asset. Predator fish are fond of using structure to search out or ambush their prey. Structure can mean many things. It can mean, of course, hard material objects like rocks, logs, or reefs; but it can also refer to less obvious things, like a spot where water clarity changes. Set yourself up so that your bow is pointing downwind in the direction that you want to travel. In most cases, this will mean pointing your bow in a direction that will take you alongside the structure you intend to target. Without a rudder, your kayak will naturally turn broadside to the wind and get blown directly downwind. If you have a rudder, you can store your paddle (in a paddle clip or under your bow bungees) and use the rudder to manage your course. Depending on the wind speed, the rudder will allow you to move 30 to 45 degrees to the right or left, while keeping both your hands free to fish. If you've set yourself up in a target-rich environment, you will be able to work a long stretch of water without ever having to pick up your paddle. We've used this method alongside other anglers who don't have rudders and watched as they constantly alternated between their paddles and rods. We can say for certain that having a rudder in play will dramatically increase the number of quality casts you can make in a day.

Joel McBride and Scott Null control their drift with rudders and silently work their way down a weed bed in Aransas Pass, Texas.

This method of controlled drifting is quite versatile. It can be employed for working your way in and out along an irregular shoreline. It works great for covering the sandy potholes of an open grass flat. And it is deadly effective for working your way down a creek and hitting every point, gravel bar, or deep pool.

Small drift anchors may also be employed in a situation where the wind is pushing you too fast. The drift anchor acts as a parachute to slow your drift and allow you to more thoroughly fish an area. You can also vary the point of attachment on your kayak to control the angle of your craft during the drift. We generally secure the drift anchor to the area just behind and to the right of the seat. This positions the kayak to drift at a slight angle and allows you to comfortably cast downwind without fear of striking the rods stowed behind your seat. Of course, a trolley anchor will work very well in this situation as well, and it will give you more control over the specific angle on your kayak as you drift. In the absence of a drift anchor, sitting side-saddle with your legs in the water will also slow your drift if you have a sit-on-top kayak. The obvious downside to doing this is that you won't be in control of your rudder if your feet aren't on the foot pegs.

Side-Saddle Fishing

Side-saddle is a very popular method for fishing from a sit-on-top kayak. While it can be used to drift fish through deeper areas, this method really shines in shallow water where you can touch the bottom. Depending on the model of kayak you own, there is usually one spot in the cockpit that is most comfortable for sitting side-saddle. Something to note is that rounded edges are easy on the legs, so when checking out kayaks you may want to test them to see how comfortable they are when sitting side-saddle.

The best way to position yourself is with your casting arm towards the bow. With all of your gear stored towards the rear of the kayak, this will give you an unobstructed cast. Because you don't have to worry about hitting anything, you can concentrate on the fishing. Another advantage to sitting this way in shallow water is that you can control your kayak without using your paddle. Simply walk your feet across the bottom and stop where you like. This method allows you to thoroughly work an area, and to fish in places where the bottom is too muddy for wading. With most of your weight being supported by the kayak, you won't sink deep into the soft bottom.

When fishing side-saddle, you're usually best off turning so that your casting arm is on the bow side of your kayak: this way, any gear in the stern won't get in your way.

Poling

Poling is not an overly popular method of kayak fishing—for obvious reasons. Standing up in a kayak takes a combination of a very stable craft, calm waters, and an excellent sense of balance. The benefit of standing up and poling is that it allows you to see down into the water for sight-casting to cruising or bedded fish. It also lets you identify important bottom features. As such, it is really only useful in areas with clear shallow water, light winds, and little current. But, when the conditions are right, it can be extremely effective. Being able to spot a fish and make a good presentation definitely increases the odds in your favor. Although you can use your paddle to pole your kayak along, some anglers prefer to use a push pole designed specifically for poling.

If you're interested in standing up and poling your kayak, make sure you get a wide kayak that is very stable. Take the kayak out to an area with a level, sandy bottom and leave all your gear in your vehicle. Chances are high that you won't get the hang of it right away, so you should be prepared to get wet. To practice, carefully get up onto your knees and stay there until you feel secure with your balance. Next try standing up slowly. If you feel off balance, just stand still. Do not try to compensate by leaning the other way. If you are in a truly stable kayak, it will right itself and settle down quickly. If you are still feeling off-balance, simply step out. It is much easier on your ego than falling out. And whatever you do, don't look straight up at a passing bird. (This is experience talking.) As a final note, make sure to avoid trying to stand in your boat over a bottom that could cause injury should you fall out.

Fishing kayaks are so stable that, in many conditions, it's possible to fish from a standing position, which gives you a better view.

Greg Bowdish stalking through the mangroves.

Wade Fishing from the Kayak

We often use our kayaks to access secluded flats and then get out. There are some situations where it just makes more sense to wade. Always use your paddle to check the depth of water and the firmness of the bottom. It is quite embarrassing and sometimes dangerous to just hop out expecting a firm bottom and shallow water, only to find yourself literally "in over your head". You have the option of simply anchoring your kayak and walking away, or you can try our preferred method. What we like to do is tie ourselves to the kayak via a bowline. This way you are bringing your trusty steed along with you and it's at the ready if the need arises to quickly relocate. A downside to tying yourself to the boat is that you have little control over where the kayak floats as you wade. It can get pretty frustrating to be wading along with the wind at your back and have the kayak getting in your way as it floats past you. A simple fix for this problem is to drop some sort of weight off the stern of your kayak and allow the weight to drag on a short rope along the bottom. We've used everything from large fishing weights to anchors tied backwards. Anything that will not actually catch on the bottom will work.

Kayak Fly Fishing

Many people who fly fish are being drawn to the kayak as a mode of transportation to get them to their favored fishing destination. Oftentimes, it only takes a short paddle trip to get you away from the drive-up wading crowd. Whether you are fishing fresh or salt, the difference between success and getting skunked can be as simple as moving a few hundred yards from where the crowd has been pounding the water. While the kayak is a fine mode of transportation for reaching your wading grounds, it can also be a very useful fly fishing platform.

A sit-inside style kayak provides the angler with a perfect place to store the stripped fly line. The front deck can be left clear of obstructions, or a mini spray skirt can be installed to facilitate shooting the fly line with minimal chance of snagging. Knowing that fly line has a mind of its own and can often hang up on the most insignificant thing, it is important to carefully check for any possible snags while rigging your kayak. If you intend to fly fish from your kayak, avoid mounting any

accessories that could interfere with the storage of your excess line. A flat, open area is essential to keeping everything moving smoothly.

The sit-on-top kayak presents its own special set of problems for fly fishing, but also has some distinct advantages. On the downside, there isn't a flat open space for your line. Fly line stripped into your lap and across your legs is just begging to hang up on something. Foot pegs, wading boots, and paddle holders are all common line-grabbing culprits. In Texas, most of our saltwater fly fishing is for redfish in very shallow water. It is a different kind of fishing, where we often spend a considerable amount of time searching out a single feeding fish in a few inches of water. These are easily-spooked creatures that will often only allow a single presentation. Nothing is more frustrating than finally getting in position for the shot, only to have it fall a few feet short of the target because the fly line snagged on a boot lace. Well, there is something more frustrating. Getting that same fish to eat your fly and then pull free when the fly line inexplicably wraps itself around the water bottle you left lying in the cockpit. Just be aware that if there is anything that could possibly tangle your fly line, it will—and it will invariably happen at the worst possible moment. To avoid the frustration, we often sit side-saddle towards the center

One of the challenges of fly fishing from a kayak is preventing your line from snagging on accessories like rod holders. This is one reason we usually don't position rod holders in front of the seat.

of the cockpit and strip excess line into the seat area, which has smooth contours and works really well as a stripping basket.

Many anglers prefer to stand in their kayak to fly fish so that they get a better look at where they're casting, and so they can cast more effectively. Of course, if you're going to do this, you'll want the widest and most stable boat available. Another option is to get pontoons, or an outrigger, for your kayak. There are a number of options now available, all of which are designed to attach to almost any type of kayak.

FFF-certified fly angler, Greg Bowdish, has spent as much time fly fishing from a kayak as anyone. "The problem with fly fishing from the kayak is not that you're low to the water; it's that you can't easily make a long casting stroke from the sitting position. To compensate for this, you need to get your body more involved," explains Greg. "The way I do this is by leaning forward as I strip the line, so that when I make my cast, I'm starting as far forward as possible. This also puts you in the best position to set the hook."

Using Bait

If you were to take a survey of anglers you'd probably find that most popular way to fish is with some kind of bait. Bait can be anything, from live species of prey, to a store-bought concoction that smells so bad you don't want to touch it without wearing gloves. We're lure-chuckers at heart, but over the years we've baited many a hook with everything from foot-long mullet, to tiny shrimp, to stinking catfish dough bait—even whole kernel corn. Obviously, there is very little extra preparation needed to use dead or inanimate bait from the kayak. Simply bring your usual gear, stow your bait where it is easily accessible, and go fishing.

Live bait is probably one of the most effective ways to catch fish. Put a hook in what the game fish naturally eat and you stand a pretty good chance of feeding some fish. The lure manufacturers are coming close, but they still can't completely reproduce Mother Nature's handiwork. The challenge with using live bait from a kayak is storing the bait and keeping it alive. Some types of live bait are simple and don't require much thought. A bucket of worms or a can of crickets can be brought along easily. Baitfish require more planning. You'll need some sort of holding tank and fresh, oxygenated water. In some cases this can be accomplished with a floating bait bucket towed alongside the kayak, although this will slow your kayak down immeasurably, so you'd better not have far to travel.

When dragging a bait bucket is out of the question, there are several other methods to consider. A bucket, small ice chest, or other type of container can be placed in the tank well while battery-operated aerators or recirculating pumps keep the baitfish inside the container alive. Several bait tanks designed specifically for use in kayaks are now on the market. Keep in mind that water is heavy and storing it in or on your kayak will change the way the kayak handles. A large amount of sloshing water could jeopardize the stability of the kayak. Use the smallest tank possible for the application. Also try using one of the gel cell batteries to power the pump. These batteries are rechargeable, relatively small and lightweight, and they will power a small pump all day. You will also need to consider how easily you can reach your bait from the seated position. Do yourself a favor and spend some time sitting in the kayak in the yard, testing your bait placement prior to heading out on the water. Perhaps the best method when using larger bait fish is to catch them as needed while on the water. This isn't always practical, but it is very handy when the bait fish are present on the fishing grounds.

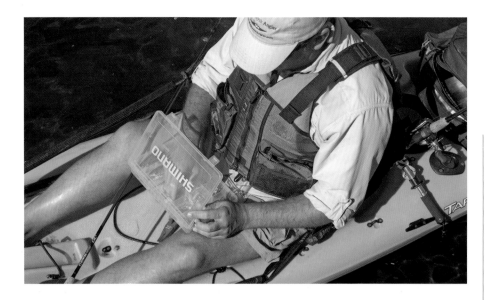

Using Lures

The biggest challenge for the lure fanatic is often in minimizing the amount of gear. For the powerboater transitioning to the kayak, this can sometimes be a real test. We all know the guy who brings along a tackle box that could double as a suitcase. If you are that guy, try to pare down your lure selection to what you actually think you'll be using. Wade and bank anglers are generally accustomed to packing light and will have no problem transitioning to the kayak. In fact, with a kayak, they'll be free to pack more gear than they would normally carry. We prefer to have one small box with a reasonable variety of lures stored within easy reach. Additional boxes with backup lures can be stowed inside the hatches, just in case you run low on the hot bait. Of course, stowing gear in hatches assumes you'll be fishing in an area where you can pull into shallow water or even to shore, so you can

step out of the kayak to retrieve your cache. If you are fishing in deep, open water then you need to have everything already within reach. Try to keep it as simple as possible. Within a few trips you'll have your own system set up.

Using Anchors

Depending on where you do your fishing, the anchor may be one of your most valuable pieces of fishing equipment. In particular, in windy or current-prone areas, the anchor lets you hold your position, so you can target a specific area. If you're attaching your anchor to a static point on your boat, we recommend clipping your anchor line to a pad eye located on the side of the kayak, just behind the seat. Clipping the anchor line to a pad eye behind the seat has the effect of turning our kayak to point down-current or downwind for easier casting. Since we both like to cast with our right arm and sit side-saddle with our legs over the left edge of our kayak, clipping the anchor line to the right edge of the kayak keeps it as much out of the way as possible. We prefer doing this over using a trolley anchor because we rarely have the need to move its position for the type of fishing we do; it doesn't make sense to add the clutter of a trolley anchor. Of course, there is definitely a time and a place for the trolley anchor as well, and some anglers make great use of them.

The great thing about the trolley anchor is that you can point your boat in whatever direction you want. By running the clip to a point at the bow of your kayak, your boat will face directly upwind, or into the current.

As you bring the clip to the center point of your kayak, it will turn more and more perpendicular to both the current and wind. As you continue towards the stern, your boat will start to face downwind or down-current. The versatility that the trolley anchor provides is truly amazing and a huge asset for some anglers. Furthermore, if you're fishing in strong current or sizable waves, the trolley anchor becomes an essential tool, as sitting in a kayak broadside to waves or strong current is very unstable. Water or waves will pile up on the side of your kayak and easily flip you. If you need to anchor in wavy conditions or strong current, you should slide the anchor clip to either the bow or stern so that your boat runs parallel with either.

With the anchor clipped to a pad eye behind the seat, the tidal current holds Joel's boat on a downstream angle, making it easy for him to cast towards the bridge pilings that he's targeting.

Fishing from a Tandem

"Can we fish from that tandem?" We get this question all the time. The answer is yes, but it isn't a great idea. The math just doesn't work. Two people in a 13- to 15-foot kayak, each armed with a 6-foot rod and a lure with multiple treble hooks, just adds up to trouble. The question usually comes from a couple, and the wife has veto power on the purchase. She's willing to go out fishing, but she's not so sure about paddling to get there. After a few minutes of explaining just how easy it is to paddle a kayak and perhaps getting her on the water for a demo, the deal is sealed. They're getting his and hers kayaks.

Even for people who want to take their kids with them, I'll usually suggest getting two kayaks instead of a tandem. With a little patience and instruction, even very young kids are perfectly capable of handling their own kayaks in protected waters. You'll both be happier.

The only time a tandem will work well for fishing is if one person is going to paddle while the other fishes. This is usually a parent with a very young child. There are also guides out there who paddle from the rear of the kayak while their client fishes from the bow. Although some will disagree, we strongly believe tandems are better suited to pleasure paddling.

Fishing with Kids

Speaking of taking the kids fishing, here's my favorite part of the book. Taking the kids outside and getting them away from the television should be every parent's goal. So many young ones are living life through others these days and not getting to experience life. I understand that it isn't easy, but nothing really worthwhile ever is. I've been taking my girls out fishing and hunting since they were just big enough to walk. In fact, I think one of them was out on a boat when she was still just crawling. Your kids are probably tougher and more resilient than you give them credit for. I know mine have constantly surprised me with what they'll put up with to be outdoors. I'm not suggesting you should push them through a grueling, 20-mile paddle, but don't underestimate them either.

Nobody knows your kids like you do. You have a pretty good idea of their capabilities and their attention span. You also know what makes them happy and what makes them whine. Use that hard-earned knowledge to plan the day. I can't tell you exactly how to pull this off, because there is a huge difference between introducing a five-year-old to fishing and trying to get your teenage daughter to spend the day with Dad.

Plan for a great day, but be prepared for the worst. By that I mean: keep them happy with enough food, drinks, and snacks; keep them comfortable with the proper clothing; and make the whole excursion fun and relaxed by keeping things simple. Have your basic first aid kit stocked and ready so you can handle unexpected emergencies calmly and effectively. Be prepared to call it a day early if the fun just isn't happening. The quickest way to ruin your child on fishing and the outdoors forever is to push them too hard and make it a miserable experience. Remember that you already have an interest in fishing, or else you wouldn't have read this book. However, your children's interest might need some cultivating; the key to that is making sure they have a good time.

With young children, it is important to have realistic expectations. Everyone dreams of getting their child hooked up with a trophy fish. The reality is that you need to set your sights a bit lower. Think back to when you were just starting out. For little kids, anything that will stretch their line or dunk their bobber will be exciting. In fresh water, this might mean putting a worm on a hook and hanging out by the docks, catching perch. In the salt you can't beat shrimp on the bottom for surefire action—and action is what you want. Save the game fish chase for later.

With very young children, you might want to think about paddling a tandem. Put them up front, where you can keep an eye on them. If they're big enough, go ahead and give them a paddle. They probably won't paddle much, but it helps make them feel like they're part of the activity. Again, don't force the issue. Provide the level of instruction and encouragement you think they can handle.

With older kids, you should consider letting them paddle their own kayak. Assess their skills and make the call whenever you feel confident they can handle it. My girls were paddling on their own as early as ten years old. Those first outings were in protected water under close supervision. I also brought along a tow rope in case of a mutiny. It is amazing how quickly they'll figure it out, and before long they're able to easily keep up. An unexpected bonus was when I realized that the girls were also happy and able to entertain themselves. Once they get bored with fishing, they'll start searching out crabs, shrimp, and other interesting critters. They have a good time exploring sea life and I have a little more time fishing.

Equip your kids for success. Get a boat that fits them, a properly sized lightweight paddle, and a comfortable PFD. Remember: keep it simple, keep it safe, and most of all, keep it fun.

Using a Powerboat as a Mothership

Although this sport is all about the simplicity of paddling a non-motorized craft, it is not always the best way to get the job done. In certain situations it just makes sense to combine a powerboat with your kayak. You can use a small boat to transport kayaks to distant shores, where it is either impractical or unsafe to paddle to them. You may also want to consider using a larger vessel as a base of operations for multi-day expeditions. Many coastal guides use their powerboats to transport kayaking clients to secluded areas that are out of reach for the average paddler. The great advantage to this strategy is that you get to fish areas that aren't often accessed.

Most often, a powerboat is used for crossing big, open water and then anchoring near some smaller backwater where the powerboat would be ineffective. The kayaks are then launched from the mothership and are free to go in search of fish. There are two basic ways to go about type of trip. One is the "hit and run"; the other is the "base camp". If you plan ahead, you'll be able to determine which style will best suit the area you are heading to.

As the name suggests, with the hit-and-run, you'll be making multiple

The combination of powerboat and kayak provides the ultimate fishing access.

stops to search for productive waters. You need to keep your rigging as simple as possible to make it easy to off-load the kayaks for quick forays into the backwaters. If the chosen location proves unsuccessful, then you bring the kayaks aboard and head for new fishing grounds. Because it is usually just a short paddle back to the boat to re-supply, there is no need to bring a bunch of gear on the kayak. Fully rigging your kayak and then reversing the process several times will seriously cut into your fishing time.

The base camp method involves a bigger commitment to a chosen fishing area. For these trips, you'll want to go ahead and bring all the supplies you think you'll need for a full day of fishing. If the group is planning on splitting up to cover more of the area, it is necessary to have a set time for the rendezvous back at the mothership. Your buddy's idea of "a full day of fishing" might not be the same as yours.

Another fun and effective way to make use of a powerboat is to have someone drop the group off at a distant location and then fish your way back to the original launch. This is similar to the river shuttle, but you're using a powerboat to get to your starting point. This method requires an honest assessment of how long it will take to get from point A to point B. You don't want to turn your fishing day into nothing more than a long paddle home. Give yourself plenty of time to leisurely fish your way back. Make that mistake and you'll end up disappointed that you had to bypass some prime fishing areas in order to get to the vehicle by the set time or before dark. It is also helpful to plan the trip with the prevailing wind at your back on the way in. (That's another lesson we learned the hard way.)

What about offshore fishing? There is great potential for playing on big water with kayaks. Targeting large offshore species from a kayak is a specialized game that requires a high level of skill and comes with quite a bit of risk. It is being done on a limited basis, but should only be considered if you are well-prepared and experienced with both your kayak and handling big fish. A mothership hovering close by is not a bad idea, should things suddenly go south. Never fish offshore alone. There are simply too many potential hazards out on the big pond.

CHAPTER 6

freshwater kayak fishing

Kayak Fishing the Great Lakes

By Chris LeMessurier

TODAY'S MODERN KAYAKS, whether SOTs or sit-insides, are a great way to enjoy fishing on your local lake or pond. A lot of the techniques already discussed in this book apply to lake fishing. Paddling strokes, paddling safety, and reentry techniques are all the same. The biggest hazard I've ever encountered on a lake is inebriated powerboaters. Remember, one of the coolest things about kayaks is that they don't draw very much water, giving you access to shallow water that powerboaters can only dream about. Stick closer to the edges of the lake whenever possible. The fishing is usually better, there's more to see, and you stand a better chance of avoiding powerboaters towing people on inner tubes. With a little knowledge of where you are going, a look at the weather forecast for the day, and some thoughtful preparation, you're all set.

In this chapter, we're going to focus our attention on kayak fishing in flowing rivers, because moving water presents new challenges and hazards to kayak anglers. We're then going to learn about some of the more challenging types of freshwater kayak fishing. In particular, we'll hear from Chris LeMessurier about kayak fishing on the Great Lakes. Chad Hoover then explains the tricks for kayak fishing for bass. Last, but certainly not least, Jamie Pistilli tells us about kayak fishing for the meanest freshwater fish of them all—the muskie.

If Rodney Dangerfield were alive today, I like to think he would move to Michigan, buy a Tarpon 140, and take up kayak fishing. He would feel right at home because kayak anglers in the Great Lakes region "don't get no respect." In other regions such as Florida, California, or Texas, kayak anglers have proven the advantages of the sport and built a large following. However, the kayak fishing boom has just begun here, and to some, the sport seems like a novel or silly idea. This is evident at just about any public boat launch where a kayak angler is setting up and launching his or her rig. It doesn't take long before someone walks up, scratches his head, and asks, "You can fish out of one of those?" The answer, of course, is yes, and all the advantages of kayak fishing in other regions hold true for the Great Lakes as well.

Places to Kayak Fish

In the Great Lakes area, there are several types of water bodies where kayak anglers can chase fish. These include inland lakes, rivers and streams, and the Great Lakes themselves.

Kayak fishing inland lakes where I live in Michigan parallels inland lake fishing in other parts of the world. Often the best lakes to fish are the ones that are difficult to access. Cue the kayak angler.

With a fishing vessel that straps to the top of a car, there's no boat launch needed. It is a huge advantage to be able to slide a kayak through the reeds and fish a lake that otherwise gets no boat traffic. Considering all the wilderness lakes of Michigan, Wisconsin, Minnesota, and Ontario, the door to fantastic inland kayak fishing is now open.

Again, kayak fishing the many rivers and streams of the Great Lakes is similar to other techniques already in practice. Just like some fancy gadget you might pull out of your tackle box, the kayak is a specialized tool. You might just use the kayak to travel between fishing locations, and then hop out on shore to actually do your fishing.

Lake Michigan, Lake Superior, Lake Huron, Lake Erie, and Lake Ontario are the Great Lakes. There are five of them, they are huge, and they are full of fish. The Great Lakes basin is home to 25 million people in the United States and 8.5 million people in Canada. Their coastline alone encompasses 10,900 miles. Although not known as popular kayak fishing destinations, the big water and big fish of the Great Lakes are attracting more and more kayak anglers each year. With little exception, trolling is the most common kayak fishing technique here. It is really just simple fishing arithmetic; an extremely large body of water + baitfish being the main forage = trolling as the most efficient technique.

Chris LeMessurier holds a salmon he caught on Lake Michigan.

Fish Targeted

Largemouth and smallmouth bass draw a lot of attention in the Great Lakes and the kayak angler cannot resist their allure. Sure, a kayaker may not be able to "run and gun" like the bass pros, but there is no better vessel to quietly slide through vast lily pad fields than a kayak.

Perhaps it's their voracious nature, their large size, or their toothy grin, but nothing gets the heart pumping like hooking a northern pike or muskellunge (muskie) from a kayak. The Great Lakes region has some of the best pike and muskie fishing in North America, and many kayak anglers have landed these beasts.

Salmon are the tarpon of the Great Lakes. Just like with tarpon, an angler can spend a whole day on the water without so much as a glance from the fish, yet there is nothing more rewarding when that strike finally comes and the fight is on. But that is where the similarity ends: tarpon go back into the water, salmon go into the cooler.

Safety

The unique risks of paddling the Great Lakes include unpredictable weather, low water temperatures, open water, high winds, and ocean-sized waves. Make no mistake, paddling on the Great Lakes can be dangerous and requires just as much preparation and attention to weather conditions as kayaking on the open ocean. If you're going to head out into exposed water, you also need to be prepared for dealing with cold water. See Chapter 7 for more on safety preparations.

Kayak anglers in the Great Lakes region are growing in numbers and starting to make some noise. Our story is a story of "yets". We don't have a large following...yet. We don't have our own kayak fishing tournament...yet. We are not a major kayak fishing destination... yet. And I think Mr. Dangerfield would agree, we don't get no respect...yet.

Kayak Fishing for Bass

By Chad Hoover

Anglers have a love affair with bass. There has probably been more written about, pondered over, and analyzed about the pursuit of the black bass family than most other species combined. No other species offers the maddening complexities or the primal simplicity. This makes them an enjoyable, lifelong pursuit for anglers of all skill levels.

There is no better way to add a sense of adventure to your bass fishing experience than to fish from a kayak, which is uniquely adept for the pursuit of this popular game fish. Far removed from the rock concert atmosphere of multimillion-dollar tournament trails, the majority of us fish for the experience—being alone in a secluded honey hole, fishing with friends or spending a day on the water with family—and it is exactly these experiences that are not only possible, but usually more enjoyable and rewarding, when fishing from a kayak.

Stealth is an oft quoted advantage, yet the kayak's benefits go far beyond sneaking in undetected. When you fish from a kayak, you see and experience things that only a non-intrusive foray into the outdoors will produce. Absent are telltale signs of human misconduct—the ever-present debris trail of aluminum cans, lure packages, bobbers, and monofilament entanglements decorating overhanging branches. This alone may indicate that you are in for an exciting outing because the fishery has little or no pressure.

Without the roar of an engine or the fierce hum of a trolling motor bushwhacking through dense vegetation, you adjust to the uncommon silence and previously muted sounds of nature. The food chain comes alive in a setting that wasn't forced into cautiousness. Seeing a baby duck dodge five subsurface explosions, a field mouse disappear in a swirl, or a small snake slithering across the surface succumb to a violent attack will cause your adrenaline to pump like nothing else.

Surprises like this will seem like a fluke at first. You will be amazed and anxious to share your experience with a fellow fisherman. After a while, you will come to understand that you are simply seeing the fish behave naturally and you'll start to expect to see these things as part of your fishing trip. This flip-flop between uncanny silence and surging adrenaline is the primary reason many kayak anglers develop or deepen their fishing addiction.

It is more than folklore or fish tales that giant bass are found in often-ignored

Chad lands a 10-pound largemouth.

There are few fishing experiences that beat having a big bass blow up on your lure.

ponds and other unassuming bodies of water. In a kayak, access to these waters is limited only to your resourcefulness, effort and willingness to suffer for the cause. Exploring and locating these waters adds an element of excitement. Some are overlooked roadside impoundments and others are forgotten oxbow lakes and flooded pastures with no access by motorized craft.

You don't often hear fishermen use words like intimacy and insight. However, these are both real benefits of using a kayak to probe the inner stretches of remote waters. Observing bass in these environments will change your idea of which lure presentations are gimmicks and which ones you should add to your arsenal. It will increase your learning curve exponentially and pay huge dividends in your bass fishing success.

Gearing Up

It's hard to go wrong choosing a kayak for bass fishing. One thing to consider is that for flipping or pitching, you'll want a kayak that allows you to stand comfortably. You just can't fish effectively if you're using all your concentration to stand up. Your fishing grounds will also dictate the kind of boat you should get. If you don't need to paddle very far to reach your favorite fishing spots, you might as well go for a

shorter and more maneuverable kayak. I use the Wilderness Systems Ride 135.

My recommendations for accessories are based on bass fishing, but apply to most freshwater species. Fishing in freshwater requires several rigging modifications that aren't as critical to success when fishing saltwater flats and marsh environments. These include mounting rod holders, proper anchor setup and deployment, and use of depth finders.

Because you are more likely to encounter overhanging brush and tree limbs, rod holders should be mounted to allow the rods to angle straight back and stay within the width of the kayak. This allows you to paddle very close to

shorelines and pass close to trees without your rods becoming entangled. This also helps keep them out of the arc of your back cast and lessens the likelihood of entanglement when fly casting.

For a long time I disliked flush-mount rod holders, but this was just because they were mounted in an awkward position. After mounting them myself to direct my rods straight back, I really like the function and the fact that they lower the rods for overhead clearance. They also work very well for accessories like lip grippers, anchors, and landing nets.

A depth finder is critical for consistently catching bass. Sure, you can beat the banks a good portion of the year, but catching big bass with any regularity

requires identifying what is going on beneath the surface. Establishing patterns during migratory periods or seasonal weather trends is nearly impossible without the use of a depth finder. To further increase your chances of success, the depth finder should be used in conjunction with topographical information, maps and GPS.

Think Like a Fish

Pre-trip planning is a must when using the kayak, since your ability to cover large expanses of water is limited. Even in the fastest models, it's impossible to cover more than a few square miles effectively. Therefore, becoming a student of the science that defines the behavior and activity of a bass is a must.

Fisheries scientists and biologists are often some of the better fishermen you will meet for one reason—they understand and can better predict the behavior patterns of the species they study. Any angler who is serious about becoming better at targeting a specific species should also acknowledge the environmental and physiological forces that affect their quarry.

After studying habitat and behavioral factors, these same considerations should be given to forage. Understanding the habits of your game fish's meal will give you another insight into predicting its location and identifying effective lure presentations. Embracing this approach to becoming a better angler will make your adventures in the kayak much more productive and rewarding.

Bait Versus Lures

Many anglers get their start by fishing live bait or natural baits as a child. This is a very effective technique and sometimes is the only real producer during daylight hours. Using artificial lures, however, is by far the most exciting method for pursuing bass from a kayak. It is both a challenging and rewarding undertaking. Plus, the ability to put the lure where you want it and impart the action you desire makes using lures more effective than natural baits in a lot of situations.

Power fishing is my favorite and most effective way to fish for bass. Big spinnerbaits, buzzbaits, topwater lures, frog baits and soft plastics are the staple of my arsenal. However, crankbaits and finesse lures both find their way into my game plan when conditions warrant.

There are few outdoor experiences that rival that of a mossy back exploding on a topwater plug, smashing a frog or slurping down a buzzbait. The black bass is a voracious predator and these techniques are effective when fished from a powerboat. However, they will be more effective, more often, when the fish are not spooky or pressured, and when you apply the insights you've gained from seeing the water from a kayak.

Kayak Fishing for Muskie

By Jamie Pistilli

What many consider to be one of freshwater's most prized and rewarding catches, the mighty muskellunge, can also be one of the most difficult and wary fish to target. When mentioning muskie angling in a kayak you may get some pretty interesting looks. However, a kayak can help bring a whole new dimension to muskie angling and offer fishermen an entirely new perspective on their favorite sport.

Finding Muskies

Kayaks let you access extremely skinny water which otherwise could not be reached by larger craft. Fish in these waters do not see as many lures and, therefore, you have a greater chance of coming into contact with them. Another great benefit of the kayak is that you can travel through and around weed beds without chewing them up with a motor. Most anglers park on a weed edge and cast parallel to it. In a kayak you can hit fish casting different angles and use various presentations that the fish are not accustomed to seeing. This will increase success.

Muskies are at the top of the food chain and you will find them in predictable spots. Finding bait on a sonar is a good start. Early season fish can be found in new weed growth or out roaming deeper water and drop-offs, searching for schools of bait.

In the cooler months, muskie can usually be found in deeper water, often off weed beds and drop-offs. Position yourself in shallow water and cast your bait into the depths and start your retrieve. In summer months when muskies are in the weeds, do not be afraid to toss large spinnerbaits and topwaters right into the thick cover; muskies will use these areas to hunt for food and take cover.

Trolling from spot to spot can also be productive. Covering a lot of water in search of active muskies is an effective way to make your day a success.

One of the massive muskie lures, with two big treble hooks on the bottom and a single hook off the top. These lures make landing a muskie more dangerous than their awesome set of teeth.

Tackle for Muskies

Heavy gear is required when fishing for these freshwater predators. It helps the angler better control the fish boat-side and is also better for the safety of the fish. A baitcasting reel is preferred because of the strong drag system and ability to hold a large amount of line. Heavy or extra-heavy action rods around 7 feet seem to work best while fishing in a kayak. Many anglers choose braided line of at least 50-pound test to fish for muskellunge and use a wire or fluorocarbon heavy leader on the business end.

Always come prepared with the proper release tools: two sets of pliers, bolt cutters, large landing net (cradles are very difficult to operate alone), and jaw spreaders. Other effective lures are topwaters, spinnerbaits, jerkbaits, and shallow-running crankbaits. Try using a lure that is easy to work with, because heavy lures can actually alter the direction of your kayak with every cast. Muskie fishing is tiring enough without the paddling involved in kayak fishing. Selecting baits that are low resistance and easy to work will save you from hitting the dock early—topwater prop baits, bucktail spinners, spinnerbaits and crankbaits all fit this bill.

While muskies will hit big baits year-round, start out with smaller baits early in the season and progress to larger baits in the fall. Many experienced muskie anglers will troll 14-inch baits in the fall.

Live Bait

Live bait is always a popular method to fish for muskies, especially in the fall. There are some live bait wells available on the market, for transporting large suckers. Keep in mind the extra water weight of the pail and bait will change the ride of your kayak.

Use a quick strike rig or a circle hook to prevent a fish from being gut hooked. In areas where you can legally use two lines, a live bait can be used near the boat and casting can draw fish in closer to find your bait if they do not find your lure appetizing.

Do not be afraid to toss or troll large bait around. A muskie can eat a meal up to 30 percent its size. Just ensure you have the proper tackle to handle these freshwater monsters.

Presentation Strategies

On pressured waters, muskies see many types of bait throughout a season. These fish tend to follow baits right to the boat and often strike just feet from the boat. If you notice a following muskie, slowly put your rod tip in the water and make

Huck a muskie lure for a day and everything else seems small.

your lure swim in a large "O" pattern. Conventional muskie anglers like to do a figure-eight pattern with their lure at the boat but in a kayak a large "O" is easier to control. When your bait is close to the kayak, press your reel's free-spool button and control the drag with your thumb rather than the drag system in the reel. This way the impact on your reel will not tip your kayak.

A general rule of thumb is "the colder the water, the slower the retrieve." This theory applies in the fall and before freeze-up, when large jerkbaits worked slowly with long pulls and fished with a large pause are an effective way to put a trophy fish in your boat. Fish tend to move around less when the water is cool and like to eat an easy meal.

In the summer season, on the other hand, you will have to reel in baits very quickly. Boat traffic, fishing pressure and forage all play a part in this theory. Muskies have a lot of energy and will chase bait down.

Muskies can also be so aggressive that they will eat a lure trolled 6–7 miles per hour directly behind a boat. Just because you are paddling in a kayak, don't think you have to run a long line for muskies. A short line is a lot easier to control for removing weeds from a fouled hook, whereas a long retrieve can throw off a good trolling run as well. Muskies are not boat-shy and even though you are paddling, your presence will not startle them. In clear water, you really want to bring in your bait fast, especially in heavily fished waters. Fish see many lures; retrieving your bait quickly can draw an impulse strike, as muskies are territorial.

When heading out, it's best to have a strategy or game plan prepared. Try rigging a few rods with baits to cover the water column. Once you get a follow or see fish activity, you can change your other rods to similar bait. A follow from a hot fish can often result in a strike and a fish in the boat.

Jamie releases a muskie he caught on the Madawaska River in Ontario, Canada.
PHOTO BY LISA UTRONKI

Landing Muskies in a Kayak

I have found working in pairs to be one of the best ways to successfully release a muskie. When netting the fish, always keep it in the water and between both kayaks, making a sort of makeshift pen. One person works on the fish, removing the hooks from the fish's mouth and untangling the line if need be, while the other angler gets the camera ready and turns the kayaks for the best photo angle in relation to the sun. Once the fish is ready, take a quick photograph or two and return the fish to the water. Muskies get extremely stressed and keeping them in the water during the hook removal process is essential for survival. As much as muskies have one mean attitude, they cannot tolerate being out of the water for long—especially in warmer temperatures.

Muskies have large teeth and can be very unpredictable—each fight is different. Some fish have massive headshakes and dive for deeper water while other fish will leap out of the water to try and free a lure.

Be prepared, have a game plan and be careful on the water and your next muskie outing in a kayak will be a great success.

Fishing Flowing Rivers

By Joel McBride

CAN I TAKE THIS BOAT ON THE RIVER?" Without more information, this question is impossible to answer. What kind of river are they talking about? I've spent 20 years of my life as an avid whitewater kayaker and have visited rivers of all shapes and sizes all over the globe. Some are suited for kayak fishing and others not. Let's take a look at the differences.

Classes of Rivers

Moving water presents a new set of challenges and obstacles. Throughout the world, rivers are rated in classes from 1 to 6. Class 1 is essentially flat water, Class 6 is unnavigable. Depending on your ability level, I think Class 1 and 2 are appropriate for kayak fishing, while all others are not.

I live along the banks of the Arkansas River, high up in Colorado. This is a well-known fishery of brown and rainbow trout and people come from all over the country to float fish it in drift boats or rafts. The best fishing is, of course, outside the high runoff and the "Ark" is a meandering Class 1 to 2 river in the prime fishing sections, when it's low. Even though I have the paddling skills to easily paddle this river, and have done so a thousand times, it's simply too busy to fish it efficiently from a kayak. You constantly have to pick up your paddle

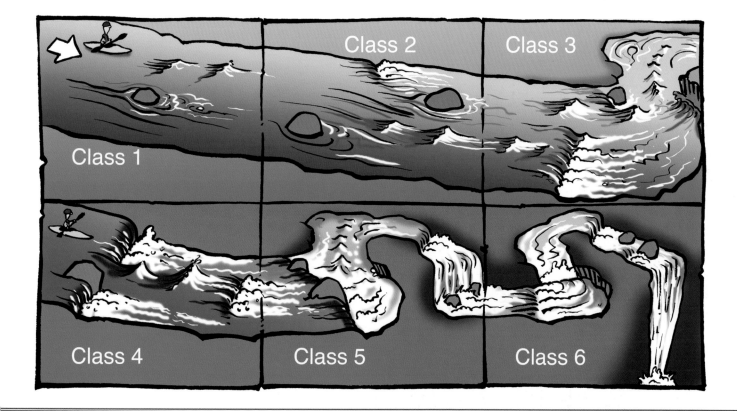

It's sometimes easiest to hop out of your kayak and fish from shore.

to make adjustments to your course and avoid hitting rocks. For rivers like this, it isn't that you don't have the skills or aren't "up to the task". It just won't be a very productive day of fishing for you; you have to choose your rivers based on what you want to do.

There are many Class 2 to 4 rivers offering less continuous whitewater and providing great kayak fishing options, albeit only for experienced whitewater paddlers. These rivers tend to be drop/pool in character, meaning that the rapids are usually caused by water spilling from one lake into another, or more generally that sections of whitewater are followed by sections of flat water. The problem with kayak fishing on these types of rivers is that, although you may have the skill to safely and reliably navigate the rapids in a whitewater kayak, by taking a loaded kayak fishing boat through the whitewater, you could easily lose all your gear. If you're interested in kayak fishing on more than Class 1 or light Class 2 whitewater, you will have to bring a lot less equipment because it will all need to be stowed and secured inside the kayak. If you are a whitewater kayaker and know what you're doing, by all means, pack a bit of fishing gear that fits in your boat and go down anything you know you can handle. You will likely do all your fishing from out of your kayak, but you'll have access to pools, eddies and small bays that may have never before seen a lure. For the sake of this book, however, we are going to ignore Class 3 and higher, and just focus on some of the things a typical kayak fisher may encounter on Class 1 and light Class 2 whitewater.

Basic Current Dynamics

Simplified, a flowing river has current and eddies. The current is the water moving downstream. Usually there's a main channel, but a midstream rock or an island can divide the main current and form multiple channels that all have current. An eddy is a pocket of water directly downstream from some form of obstruction, for example, a rock or a part of the river bank that juts out. The deflection of water by the obstruction creates a relatively calm area below—a paddler's parking spot. The concept is quite simple. When water is deflected by an object, it's pushed away from one area and towards another, creating a differential in the amount of water between the two areas. Because of gravity, the river naturally wants to equalize this differential by flattening itself out. To achieve this, the water circles back into the area that it was originally deflected away from. The result is an eddy on the

downstream side of the obstruction. This flow creates an upstream current (from bottom to top) in the eddy that can vary in strength from being almost unnoticeable (on gentle, slow rivers) to very powerful (on fast-flowing, big-volume rivers). An eddy line forms where the upstream-flowing water of the eddy (the eddy current) meets the downstream-flowing water of the river (the main current), creating a helical (whirlpool-like) flow that is usually fairly easily distinguishable as a rough line. The eddy line is narrowest and most crisply defined at the top of

the eddy and it dissipates toward the bottom of the eddy.

Something else to consider is that water in motion carries incredible momentum. One of the results of this momentum is that when a river bends, a lot of water will get pushed to the outside of the turn, where it will then be deflected into the right direction. This is very important for a kayaker to understand because it means that if you were to float down the middle of a flowing river, you would get taken to the outside of a bend, along with most of the river's water. This is where the

Brendan Mark sits comfortably in the calm water of the eddy, just on the outskirts of the main current.

current will be fastest, the waves the biggest, and this is also where debris such as fallen trees will end up (which are a very real hazard). On the inside of a bend, the water will be flowing much more slowly. Obviously this will impact how you navigate down a flowing river. It doesn't mean that you'll always want to hug the inside of a corner, but it certainly means that this is a good default course to take.

Getting to the Fish—Paddling in Current

By Ken Whiting

Now that you understand basic river dynamics, let's look at the practicalities of kayak fishing in flowing rivers before we look at some of the hazards. As any river angler knows, fish love to hang out in eddies and wait for the main current to bring the food to them. Experienced

kayakers can use the kayak to get to spots on rivers that are otherwise inaccessible to other anglers. That may simply be the eddy on the other side of a popular fishing river. In order to get to that eddy safely (and upright), there are a few things that you need to know about paddling in current.

As we mentioned at the beginning of this segment, for the purposes of kayak fishing, we're only considering Class 1

Ken Whiting prepares to pull out of the current and into an eddy.

rapids—or at most Class 2. With that said, even light current is incredibly powerful and needs to be respected. So, first things first. If you're going to paddle in current, be sure to safely stow any gear on the deck of your kayak. Your boat can capsize very quickly in even the mildest current and the only thing worse than a damaged ego is broken or lost gear.

As a general rule, your goal when paddling through current is to spend the least amount of time on eddy lines. Often, you can just point your boat downstream or upstream and paddle, staying in the main current and avoiding eddy lines altogether. Keeping your boat straight and your body forward, you can paddle through some pretty big waves this way. Other times though, there will be an enticing eddy on the side of the river that you want to reach, so we're going to take a look at the two basic techniques for working your way in and out of eddies.

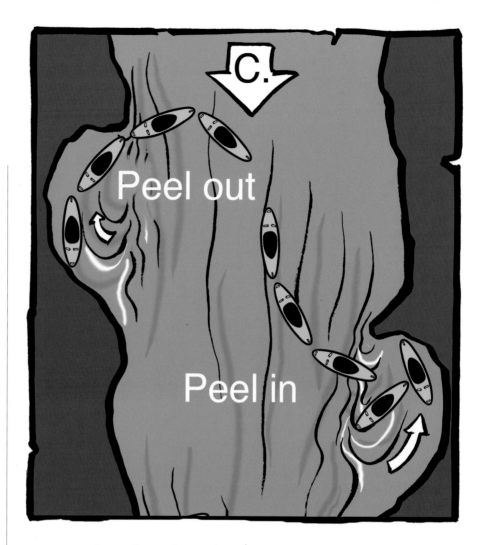

EDDY TURNS

Crossing an eddy line into or out of an eddy is called an eddy turn. It's also referred to as *peeling* in and out, or *eddying* in and out. The first thing to know is that when crossing into the main current from an eddy, you always want to cross the eddy line with your boat on about a 45-degree angle pointing upstream or up-current. It is very important that you

carry some forward speed into this maneuver, because you want to cut across the eddy line decisively and not end up stranded in the confused water between the two currents.

As soon as your bow crosses the eddy line, the main current will grab it and pull it downstream. If you're not prepared for this, it can flip your boat. The way to prepare yourself is to tilt your boat downstream as you cross the eddy line, just as you'd lean a motorcycle into a corner.

Using this technique you should be able to carve a smooth turn into the main current.

If you are moving from the main current into an eddy, you'll use the same technique. The only difference is that you will want to cross the eddy line with your bow on a 45-degree angle towards downstream. As soon as your bow crosses the eddy line, your boat will get turned upstream, so you need to prepare yourself by tilting your kayak into the turn.

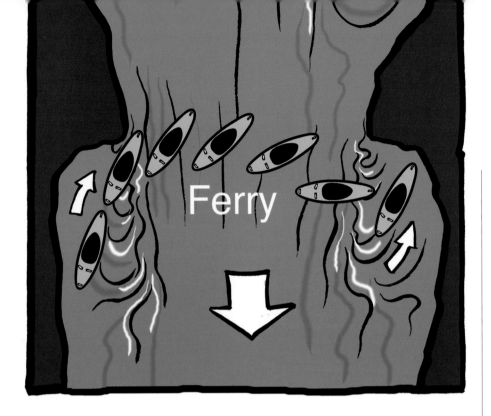

FERRYING

The ability to use current to help you get where you need to go will transform your ability to maneuver in moving water. The most basic means of doing so is called a ferry.

Ferrying is a technique used to cross current laterally, and is accomplished by paddling with your kayak angled upstream so that during your crossing, you make enough upstream progress to counteract the speed at which the current is pulling you downstream. In milder current, you can point yourself more directly across to your destination, but when the current gets stronger, you'll have to keep a fairly aggressive upstream angle on your kayak to fight the current that will otherwise pull you downstream. If the current is strong and

there are waves to contend with, you'll also need to keep your boat tilted on a slight downstream angle throughout your ferry. This ensures that water doesn't pile up on the upstream edge of your kayak and flip your boat.

If you're starting your ferry from an eddy, you'll want to cross the eddy line like you did for an eddy turn, but with a bit more upstream angle, so your bow doesn't get pulled downstream. As you cross the eddy line, you may need a few sweep strokes on the downstream side of your boat to keep your bow pointed upstream.

HANDLING ROCKS

When dealing with Class 1 and 2 current, the chances are quite low that you'll encounter rocks, but it's important

to know what to do if the situation does arise. When being carried towards a rock in current, your best option is obviously to turn and paddle away from it; but if it can't be avoided, you need to take actions that will probably fight your natural instincts. The natural response to colliding with a rock is to turn sideways and lean away from it, which puts your kayak between yourself and the rock. Unfortunately, this action will have some very undesirable results, as leaning away from the rock means leaning upstream. As soon as your kayak hits the rock, current will pile up on your upstream edge and flip you mercilessly. So what should you have done?

When drifting into a rock that can't be avoided, you need to keep your boat tilted downstream to prevent your upstream edge from catching the main current. In lighter current, or when dealing with lower-angle, rounded rocks, this might simply mean holding an edge and bouncing into the rock. You might even have to push yourself laterally off the rock with your downstream hand. In faster current, or when the rock is more vertical, you may need to lean your whole body into the rock while holding your boat on edge. You may also need to push yourself laterally off the rock quite aggressively with your downstream hand. Of course every situation is different, but the key is always to keep your upstream edge

from catching water. Lean into the rock and give it a big (but gentle) hug!

Rocks that are just below the surface can also wreak havoc on unsuspecting paddlers and are common causes of broken paddles. With experience, there's no reason to get caught by surprise by such a rock, as your river reading skills will allow you to recognize them early on. If your path does take you over a submerged rock, you should try to hit the rock as straight on as possible, with enough speed to drive over top of it. This is a good reason to keep your kayak fairly straight with the current in the early learning stages—before your river reading skills have developed.

SWIMMING IN CURRENT

There are two ways of swimming through a rapid. You can swim defensively or offensively. Defensive swimming is also referred to as "body surfing" and involves floating downstream in a protected position: lying on your back, feet downstream, arms out to the side and with your whole body floating as close to the surface as possible. This is the best swimming position to assume if your goal is to ride out a rapid or if you're in shallow water and worried about hitting rocks.

If you need to actually get somewhere, you'll adopt the offensive swimming technique. Offensive swimming involves getting on your stomach and swimming hard with the front crawl.

The body surfing position keeps your whole body as close to the surface as possible.

River Hazards and Safety

Moving water, even slow-moving water, is a powerful force. Just as important as being able to read the water to know where to cast, you need to be able to read the water to know what it's doing and where it's going. This is a critical part of identifying hazards so you can avoid them. Paddling and fishing on flowing rivers are two of my favorite activities. With a little common sense and forethought, they can be done very safely.

STRAINERS

Strainers are probably the most common and dangerous obstacles on any river. A strainer is a pile of logs or other debris that has been stacked up by the current over time, usually against a rock or bridge abutments. They are called strainers because they work just like pouring pasta and hot water into a colander. The pasta is stopped by the colander while the water passes through the holes. With a strainer on the river, a kayak can get pinned like the noodles against the strainer while the water passes through. The difference is that the water never stops flowing on the river, and the longer you and your boat are pinned there, the worse it gets. It can be extremely dangerous to get caught against a strainer—even in what

Experienced whitewater kayakers Brendan and Joel run through a Class 2 rapid. Notice the thigh straps they use for extra boat control, and that their fishing gear is all safely stored in the kayak.

you think is fairly light current—and if you get pulled under, rescue can be near to impossible. If your kayak gets pinned and you can still get yourself out and on to land, it is often wise to consider abandoning your boat and get help later to pull it out. A boat and gear can be replaced—you can't. Of course, the best thing to do with strainers is to identify them from upstream and give them a wide berth; completely avoid them from the start.

A strainer lets water through, but stops bigger objects... like you!

LOW HEAD DAMS

Low head dams are an extremely hazardous obstacle on the river. For starters, they are very difficult to see from upstream until it is too late. Because a low head dam is man made, it is built with a perfectly horizontal pour-over line, causing it to form a perfect hydraulic on the other side. Among fire departments and river rescue circles, low head dams are referred to as "drowning machines." The only plan of attack here is to know whether the river you are paddling that day has one on it or not. If it does, know where it is, take out well above it, and portage to a spot well below it before putting back in. Leave nothing to chance with a low head dam. Have a plan and stick to it.

FOOT ENTRAPMENT

The foot entrapment is one of the most common causes of death in shallow, moving water. When you're standing up in current, your foot can get lodged between rocks or anything else on the riverbed. With your foot stuck, the current can easily knock you over and even a light current can make it impossible to get up or unstuck. Foot entrapments can easily lead to a drowning in as little as two feet of water. Being a good swimmer is irrelevant. Avoiding a foot entrapment is easy—simply don't wade out into fast moving water. If for some reason you do find yourself swimming in fast-moving current, resist the temptation to stand up and walk to shore, even if you're in only a few feet of water. Swim your way right into shore and out of the main current before you attempt to stand.

USING ANCHORS

In kayak fishing, anchors are a popular way to keep your boat in one spot. Generally speaking though, anchoring in moving water is a very bad idea. If you must, make sure you do it from either the bow or stern of the boat so that your kayak is held parallel to the current. If your anchor is clipped closer to the center of your kayak, your boat will sit more perpendicular to the current, which lets water "pile up" on your upstream side and try to flip you. If you are going to experiment with anchoring in moving water, make sure you bring along a knife so you can cut the line quickly if you have to.

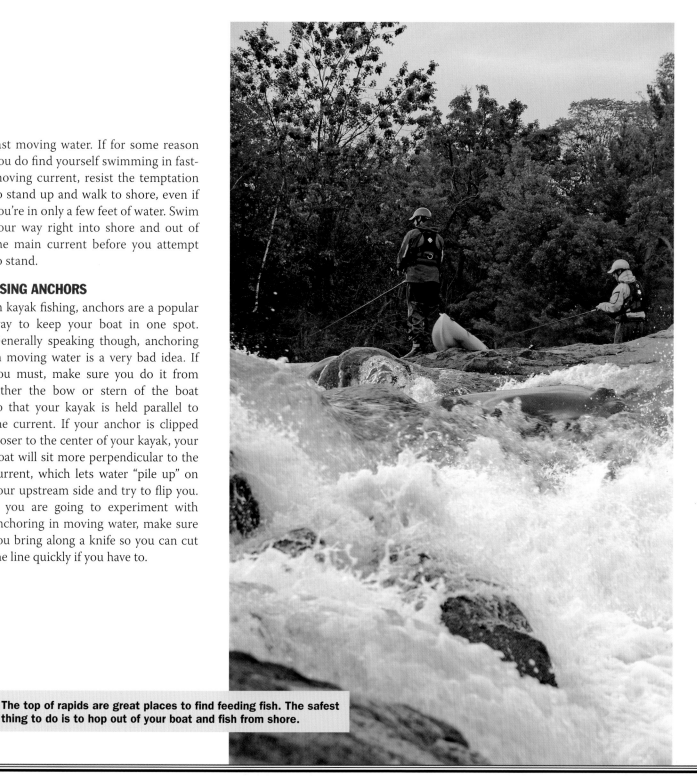

The top of rapids are great places to find feeding fish. The safest thing to do is to hop out of your boat and fish from shore.

saltwater kayak fishing

Understanding Tides and Tidal Currents

If you plan on doing any kayak fishing in saltwater, you need to have an understanding of tides and tidal currents because they can have a profound impact on your paddling and fishing plans. The first thing to understand is that there is a difference between tides and tidal currents. Tides are the vertical movement of water up and down, while tidal currents are the horizontal movements of the water. Tides and tidal currents result from the gravitational effects of the moon on the earth's oceans. As such, tides are predictable in both height and strength of current based on the position and phase of the moon as well as the time of year. There are tide tables available for every part of the world that provide the tide level as well as the amount of flow.

There are a few terms you need to become familiar with in order to begin to understand how tides will affect your fishing. Flood tides are when the water is rising. Ebb tides are when the water is dropping. The high tide is when the water is at its highest and low tide is when the water is at its lowest. Simple enough, but that is just the beginning.

The commonly available tide charts will provide you with information about the height of the water at a given time, in a given place. Tides vary greatly throughout the world, with some locations having twenty or more feet of difference between the high and low, while other places will have less than a foot of change. The tide level can be crucial to choosing an area to fish, depending on the species of fish you are seeking. Local knowledge is priceless when it comes to predicting where the fish will be on a given tide.

Although in some areas tides can have a dramatic effect on water levels, tidal currents will usually play a bigger part in locating feeding fish. For any tidal change, there is a time of maximum flood, when the water is flooding in at its greatest speed, and a time of maximum ebb, when water is flowing back out at its greatest speed. Between the flood and ebb times there are periods when the movement slows or even stops and then resumes, called "slack tide". As an angler, you are looking for the periods when the current first begins moving, or just before it stops moving. These are often the times when the bite really turns on. Moving water causes nature's food store to come to life. Slack tide is dead water and there will be very little feeding activity during that time. It is also true that the fishing will sometimes shut down when the current is at its strongest.

On a recent trip to Tampa Bay, the effects of water movement on fish were very clearly illustrated to us. It was dead low tide, with no movement. We had parked the kayak and were walking an exposed sandbar. Several big fish were visible, lying nearly motionless in the scattered sand potholes of the grass beds. These fish refused every lure that we danced right in front of them. It was tough to sit there looking at these huge redfish and snook, knowing they weren't going to bite. After a while, the standing grass began to waver as the tidal flow slowly started to move. Within minutes those same fish were feeding and consistently taking the very same lures that they had previously snubbed. It was a dramatic and obviously tide-influenced incident.

Something that is often overlooked in all of the tide talk is the wind. Wind-driven currents are sometimes as useful as tidal currents. On our flats in

Texas, we'll often have less than a foot of difference between the high and low tide. Spread this out over the several hours between the high and low tides and you will understand that there is very little tidal current being produced. In situations like these, seek out the wind currents. The wind pushes the water across the open areas and piles water against the far shoreline. Any islands or breaks in the shoreline will funnel these wind currents and accelerate them to the point that they become useful for locating fish.

The old salts had far less information at their disposal than we do today and were much more in tune with the ways of nature. They almost instinctively understood how the tides worked and what effects they would have on the fishing. Today, we have tons of information at our fingertips. Within a few minutes on a computer, we can know about the tide, current, water temperature, and the weather conditions—without ever even going near the water. While all of this information is great, you still need to learn how it applies to your area and the fish you seek. There is no way we could cover every species and every situation that you may encounter within the scope of this book. That is your homework assignment. It is a lifelong study that can be as entertaining as the fishing itself.

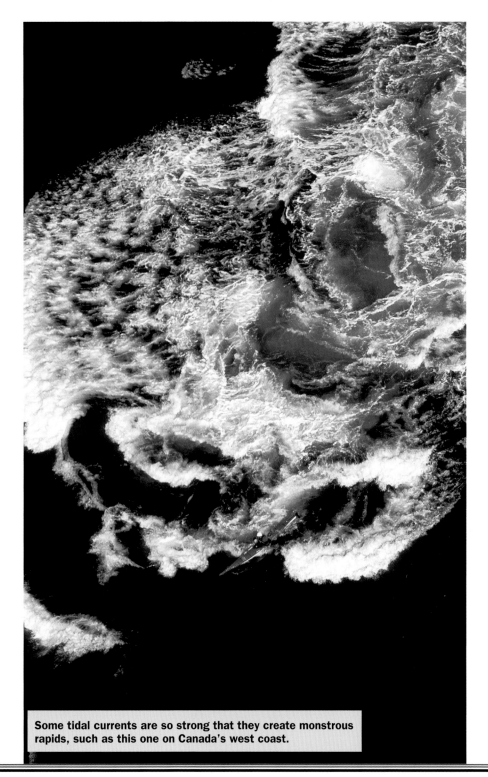

Some tidal currents are so strong that they create monstrous rapids, such as this one on Canada's west coast.

Dealing with Surf

By Ken Whiting

If you want to fish beyond a surf zone, you need to figure out a system for safely stowing all your gear so that if you were to capsize, you wouldn't have to worry about losing anything. You'll also have to learn how to paddle out through the breakers or paddle in through them to a beach landing, which can be challenging and also potentially dangerous because of hazards like rip currents. So, if you plan on paddling in an area that requires navigating through surf, it's a very good idea to take surf/sea kayaking lessons. Surf kayaking lessons will teach you how to launch, break out through waves and then land again. They'll also let you know how to deal with different rescue situations that could arise.

In this segment, we're going to start by looking at the difference between a friendly and dangerous surf zone, and then look at the basics of paddling in a surf zone.

Choosing a Beach

Surf zones are funny. Some surf zones can be considered the most entertaining natural playgrounds ever, while other surf zones are as close in character to a playground as a toxic waste dump.

The first thing to know is that surf waves are formed when ocean swell hits shallower sections of water. If the transition to shallower water is abrupt, as it often is with an offshore reef, the waves will grow quickly and then dump hard. If the transition to shallow water is gradual, the waves will rise slowly and break with less ferocity. You can probably see why

the safer surf zone involves a nice, sandy beach with a long, gradual slope. It also makes a huge difference if this surf zone is not subject to the direct impact of an ocean's swell. This means that somewhere in between the beach and the great wide ocean, there is a reef, shoal, or island(s) to absorb some of the energy of the ocean swell as it rolls into shore.

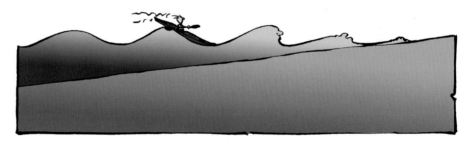

Gradually sloping beaches create milder surf, while steep beaches tend to generate dumping surf.

Rip currents are channels of current traveling directly out to sea. They can be helpful for paddling out, but dangerous for swimmers.

A less obvious factor in dictating the "safety factor" of a surf zone is the presence of rip tides. A rip tide is formed because the nature of some beaches allows waves to force more and more water up the beach and trap it there. This trapped water is now higher than the ocean level, and so it's desperately looking for a way to get back down. Once it finds an opening back out to sea (usually a deeper channel in the surf zone), all that trapped water will rush towards it and a rip tide is formed. These rip tides can result in very powerful current traveling directly out to sea. Experienced surfers will sometimes use rip currents as conveyor belts to get out past the choppy shore break, but unprepared swimmers can get caught in rip currents and swept out to sea—a dangerous situation to find yourself in. Since rip currents are usually fairly narrow channels of current traveling directly out to sea,

the best way to escape their grasp is to swim perpendicular to shore. As you can probably imagine, swimmers who don't understand the nature of rip currents often try swimming directly back to shore, which means they're only fighting the current—a battle they are almost guaranteed to lose.

Most rip currents are well known by the locals, and surf zones with rip tides are usually marked as such by signs. Of course, if you don't know the area in which you're going to be paddling, it's only prudent to ask someone who does.

Kayaks for Surf Zones

There is a wide range of fishing kayaks that work well in surf zones. Sit-on-top fishing kayaks are best because they are stable, they self bail, and they won't swamp if you end up flipping. You can also just climb back in if you fall out. A less common fishing kayak that can be used in surf zones is the sea kayak (with the use of a skirt). Sea kayaks deal with surf better than sit-on-top kayaks because they are long and narrow, which lets them slice through the oncoming waves. Of course, unless you're experienced and know how to roll a sea kayak, the sit-on-top kayak is your only option. The sit-on-top also provides a much

better fishing platform once you're out past the break—which is why the vast majority of anglers use them.

The only kayaks that you shouldn't bring into surf zones are recreational sit-inside kayaks. The problem with these boats is that the first big wave you encounter will swamp your kayak and then probably flip you. You're then stuck with a heavy, swamped boat in the midst of breaking waves. Not only is this a pain in the butt to deal with, but it's a real hazard to you and to anyone else who is using the beach.

Launching in Surf

Launching in surf can be pretty tricky because waves will be constantly washing up the beach and knocking your gear around. Regardless of the type of kayak you have, take advantage of the fact that waves come in sets with lulls in between, and that there are usually spots along a beach where waves are breaking with less impact than others. Once you've chosen your spot, watch the waves and time things so that you're launching and paddling out during the lull between sets.

Take your time when launching in surf. Wait for a lull between sets and identify where the waves are breaking the least.

To launch a sit-on-top kayak, the easiest thing to do is to point your kayak directly into the oncoming waves and drag your kayak into a foot or two of water (with all your gear stowed). You'll then wait until a wave passes and then hop onto your boat and start paddling directly out into the oncoming waves. If you're using a sea kayak it's not going to be this easy. Even if you do have the balance to slide into your kayak while it's floating (which is very difficult to do) you almost assuredly won't have the time to get your skirt on, which means the first wave that hits you will swamp your kayak. For sea kayaks, the best place to get into your kayak is on the beach, in a place where one of the bigger waves will wash enough water up its slope to lift you off the sand and let you paddle out. When you decide the time has come, climb in and get your skirt on as quickly as possible. Make sure to align your boat directly into the oncoming waves as you do this and slide your paddle under the deck lines, so it doesn't get washed away. You'll probably now have to push yourself out with your hands.

When launching, hold the bow of your kayak directly into the waves. As soon as you get a calm moment, hop in and start paddling.

Once you've launched and you're on the move, keep your eyes on the oncoming waves and try to choose a path that avoids the breaking waves. If a breaking wave is unavoidable, the best place to hit it is where it first broke, as it will have released more of its energy. The worst time to hit a breaking wave is when it has just peaked and started to dump, because it will be steepest and will pack the most wallop. Either way, to get through a breaking wave, you'll need some good forward speed, while keeping your boat pointed directly into it. It also helps to dig a last stroke into the wave as it hits you. This stroke keeps you balanced and pulls you through the wave.

Launching in surf can be pretty tricky and very intimidating, although it's actually easier than it might initially seem. In fact, it comes as a surprise to many to hear that it's easier to paddle out through moderate surf than it is to come back through it to land on the beach. The key is keeping your boat perpendicular to the waves and paddling hard directly at them. With an aggressive approach like this, you'll be amazed at the waves that you can punch through.

To punch a breaking wave, paddle hard directly at it, keep your weight forward, and plant a powerful last stroke to pull yourself through. It also helps to tuck your head behind your top arm to shield your face from the wall of water.

Even in tiny surf you need to hop right out of your boat, grab the bow, and pull your kayak up the beach.

Landing in Surf

Landing in surf is a lot more difficult than paddling out, so take your time and be sure to stow all your gear (don't forget your hat and sunglasses either!). Remember that waves come in sets and there are often spots along the beach where waves are less powerful, so take the time to watch and learn the rhythm and pattern of the waves as they roll in before making your move.

Once you make your move to shore, you have two choices. You can surf a wave into shore, or you can chase a wave into shore. Chasing a wave means following on the heels of the last wave in a set. By chasing a wave you don't need to worry about controlling a front surf and losing control of your kayak. With experience, you'll likely end up using a combination of the two by surfing the wave into shore until a point just before it starts breaking. You'll then slam on the brakes with some aggressive back strokes and then chase that same wave right into shore. Either way, the key to staying upright is staying square to the waves.

Once you reach shore, don't relax too quickly. Your boat will get beaten around by the shore break unless you hop out, grab the bow, and drag it up the beach. The more loaded your kayak is with gear, the more careful you'll have to be. Not only will a heavier boat be harder to control, but if it does get away from you it can really hurt you or someone else.

If you're on shore helping other anglers land their kayak, make sure you give their boats a wide berth and don't stand directly in front of one, try to catch one, or position yourself between a kayak and the shore. It's amazing how much of a wallop a little kayak can pack when it's being pushed around by waves!

Jim Sammons takes the more aggressive landing option and surfs the wave right into shore. Notice how aggressively he's leaning his kayak into the wave to prevent himself from getting flipped into the beach.

Saltwater Fishing Hazards and Safety

In the saltwater environment, it seems at times that almost everything out there is trying to get you. From sharks to rip currents to unseen bacteria, it can be somewhat intimidating.

Every outdoors activity has its challenges and inherent dangers. Paddling and fishing in saltwater presents a unique set of problems that you must be aware of and be prepared to deal with. This is not meant to frighten or alarm anyone. The last thing we want to do is discourage anyone from venturing into the bays or oceans. However, going into any situation with a complete knowledge of the possibilities will keep you safer than if you just pretend that those dangers do not exist. Fear of the unknown keeps far too many people from experiencing life. This section is intended to educate you to the possible dangers and hopefully make your trip to the coast safe and enjoyable.

Sharks

When inlanders talk about fishing at the coast, the issue of sharks usually comes up. Shark bite incidents are extremely rare and usually involve some sort of situation where the shark has confused a person for baitfish. The vast majority of sharks are nothing more than a nuisance to anglers, if they even show themselves at all. Yes, there are localized areas where sharks are a problem, but for the most part there is little to worry about. The highest risk for an encounter exists when you cart around a stringer of fish, which is fairly self-explanatory. To avoid having problems in areas known to have lots of sharks, simply carry a fish bag along and store your catch in there. The second highest risk is in having a shark become interested in the fish struggling at the end of your line. If the "Grey-Fin Express" decides to take your fish at a distance, it's just a disappointing turn of events. Should that same shark decide the time to eat your fish is at the same moment you try to land it, now you've got a problem. An effective way to avoid this situation is to pay attention to what is going on around your kayak as you reach for the fish. A shark will usually circle around its intended prey before it strikes. If you've become entranced by the fish on the end of your line, it could lead to quite a surprise. Stay aware of your surroundings and you'll probably see the shark before it becomes a problem.

Stingrays

Probably the second most frequent fear is of stingrays. Rays have a self-defense mechanism built into their tail in the form of a detachable barb. When threatened, rays whip their tails up over their backs and plant their barbs into whatever is above them. If you step down onto a ray, you'll likely get a nasty wound. There are ray guard boots and shin guards available to help protect you from the barb, but avoiding the encounter is by far the safest. Short of remaining in the kayak and never setting foot on the bottom, the best way to avoid having a ray encounter is to shuffle your feet. A ray will move out of the way to avoid you if he knows you're coming. Many people who have been struck by rays were hit when they stepped backwards to the hook or while fighting a fish. As bottom feeders, rays are attracted to the disturbed bottom and will often follow you around as you wade. Don't be alarmed. It isn't stalking you, it's just doing its thing. Just don't inadvertently step backwards onto it while it's at the dinner table. If you are unfortunate enough to get struck by a ray, place a hot water compress on the wound and immediately seek medical attention. Do not use ice on the wound! The poison in the barb is protein-based and ice will only make it hurt more. Heat will not eliminate the pain, but it will make it bearable. A thorough cleaning of the wound and a round of antibiotics are necessary because of the nasty bacteria these guys carry around.

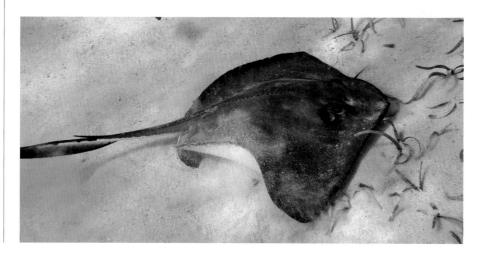

Other Creatures

In addition to the "big two" (sharks and rays), there are numerous other creatures to be aware of. Fish can bite, or poke you with a fin, and any number of other creatures such as oysters, barnacles, and sea urchins can cause a cut or puncture wound. The biggest threat from a wound in saltwater is from bacterial infection. There are some really nasty bacteria out there in the saltwater environment. It is imperative to clean and treat any wound as soon as possible and then keep an eye on it for any signs of an infection. Should an infection or fever arise, immediately seek medical attention. Some of these bacteria are nothing to laugh about and can cause serious health issues.

Weather

Creatures are usually the cause of the most angst to those new to saltwater, but weather and water pose the greater threat to the unprepared angler. If you plan to fish in saltwater, you need to appreciate how quickly and powerfully the conditions can change. High winds, waves, thick fog, and thunderstorms can develop with very little warning in this environment. Your best defense is to study the weather before hitting the water and then vigilantly observe changing conditions while you are there. Many people get caught up in all of the fun and fail to pay attention to the brooding clouds on the horizon. Remember the handheld VHF radio we talked about earlier? Most of these have a weather band channel that allows you to listen to updated forecasts and weather warnings from the NOAA. It is a good idea to carry the radio and turn it on every now and then to check on the conditions.

Tides and Currents

Tidal flows and levels can also pose a problem for the unprepared. Currents can abruptly change direction between the ebb and flood. At best, this could leave you with a tough paddle back to your launch. At worst, it could become life threatening. You don't want to get caught in a channel during a strong outgoing tide. The funneling effect of the constricted channel will accelerate the current, leading to a potentially dangerous situation. A paddle craft is no match for the strong tidal flows of ocean passes. During these tide changes, the water levels can radically change the terrain that you have to deal with. A low tide can expose reefs and rocks, cause channels to run dry, or reveal mud flats that leave you stranded far from the water's edge. High tides can cover beaches as well as landing and launch sites, and the changing landscape can

make you seriously disoriented. The bottom line is that if you're new to an area, ask around to find out about the tide and if there is anything you need to be aware of. Know your tide charts and plan your day accordingly.

Although many access points will identify potential hazards like rip tides and surf waves, it's worth asking the locals about the best and safest places to fish.

Currents off the beach don't necessarily follow the tide charts and are something to be aware of out on the open ocean. Although most people associate current with flowing

rivers or channeled areas of the inland waterways, open ocean currents can be quite strong. If you intend to fish off the beach, please study the available charts and predicted currents. Getting pushed away from shore by strong current is a deadly serious ordeal that isn't worth all the fish in the ocean. At beaches, waves can cause strong offshore flows referred to as rip currents. Rip currents are the primary cause of swimmer rescues at surf beaches because they can be tricky to spot and are surprisingly powerful. These currents form when water that has been pushed up on a beach by breaking waves retreats to the open

water. Because waves continually push more water up the slope of the beach, there can be a lot of water searching for the quickest way back out, and strong ones can take you a lot farther out than you imagined or planned. Should you ever get caught in a rip current, the way to escape it is to move perpendicular to the current until you're free. Fortunately, public beaches that are subject to strong rip currents usually have lots of warning signs and are well known by the locals. If you do decide to launch from the beach, keep in mind that for other beach users, you're going to be the biggest hazard! When caught in a wave, your kayak becomes a plastic torpedo and can really hurt other swimmers.

The Other Guy

The final danger is "the other guy". This applies to both fresh and saltwater. You are no match for a powerboat, or even a small sailboat. We understand that in most situations you do have the right-of-way because you are in a human-powered vessel, but that is not what you want chiseled onto your tombstone: "He had the right-of-way." You need to be alert and cautious while in areas frequented by other boaters. Boat wakes and inattentive drivers can ruin your day. You must realize that while sitting in a kayak, you are fairly low to the water and can be somewhat difficult to see in some situations. I don't want to give a boater any excuse for not knowing I'm there. Brightly colored kayaks, clothing, and paddles will all make you more visible on the water. Some people have begun to place brightly colored "bicycle flags" on their kayaks to increase their visibility. It is also a good idea to keep some type of noise signaling device close by. Some people carry a small air horn that can get attention from a long distance.

Kayak Fishing Florida

By Greg Bowdish

Over the past few decades, kayak fishing has evolved into as many different sports as there are species of fish. Whether it is bottom fishing offshore over a wreck, stalking tailing bonefish with a fly rod, or simply spending a lazy day bass fishing on a small farm pond, the kayak has proven both its mettle and its versatility. So, imagine having that versatility in a place that bills itself as "The Fishing Capital of the World", with over a thousand miles of coastal shoreline and a seemingly endless array of rivers, lakes, streams, marshes, swamps, and canals. It is no wonder that kayak fishing has exploded in popularity in the state of Florida.

When we talk about kayak fishing in Florida, versatility is the key word. No matter where you are in the state, you are rarely more than an hour from the coast and probably could find decent fishing within a few miles. Fishing could mean anything from largemouth bass to redfish, to permit, to peacock bass, to tarpon, to even pelagic species

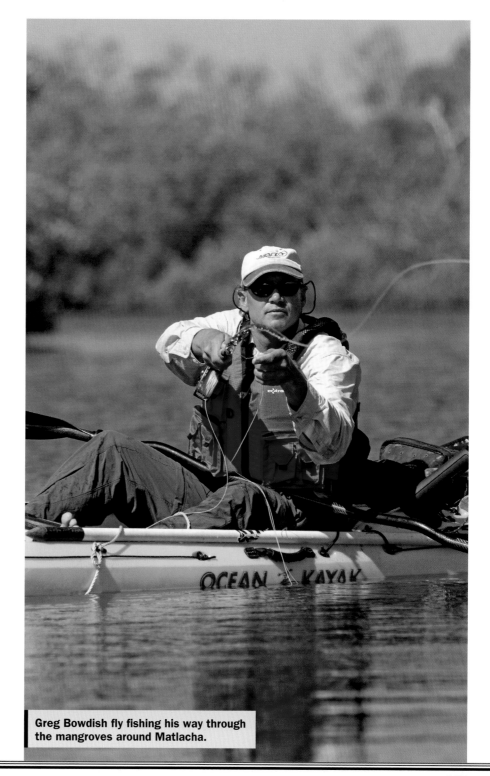

Greg Bowdish fly fishing his way through the mangroves around Matlacha.

like bonito and sailfish. And getting to your quarry could entail launching your kayak through heavy surf, navigating a twisting maze of mangroves, racing the tide through expansive salt marshes, or finding a hidden launch spot behind an urban shopping center. And this is just scratching the surface of the crazy and diverse situations you can get into with a kayak and a fishing rod in Florida. There seems to be only one rule of thumb: whatever the fish and whatever its habitat, the kayak is an excellent way to get there.

East Coast

The entire east coast of Florida, from Fernandina Beach in the north to Miami Beach in the south, offers fantastic beach fishing opportunities for many species including kingfish, Spanish mackerel, tarpon, cobia, jack crevalle, and sharks. Getting to the fish means crossing the surf zone, so make sure you've had some practice surfing your kayak before you load it with your fishing gear. Even if the surf is light when you go out, it doesn't necessarily mean that it will be that way when you come in. Thigh straps are a good thing to have along, and wearing a good-quality, comfortable PFD is a must. Fishing techniques range from live-baiting to trolling plugs and spoons, to sight-fishing, to busting fish with artificials and bait. The fishing can be good year-round depending on species, but in the winter months the surf can be very rough.

The east coast also offers a wide variety of inshore kayak fishing for such species as redfish, seatrout, flounder, jack crevalle , tarpon, and snook. From expansive salt marshes in the north to mangrove backcountry in the south, there's a wide variety of habitats and fishing possibilities. Topwater plugs, weedless spoons, soft plastics, and flies make up the arsenal of most inshore kayak anglers on the east coast. One of the most notable places for kayak fishing

is the area comprising the Indian River, Banana River, and Mosquito Lagoon in the central part of the state. Less than an hour from Orlando and Disney World, this fishery offers clear water and year-round opportunities for a variety of species including huge redfish, seatrout, and tarpon. It is also the home of Cape Canaveral, which makes it a great destination for a family vacation.

The cast coast offers some unique freshwater opportunities as well. From January through March, in the northeast end of the state, American shad run up the St. Johns River. These sea-run members of the herring family can reach 8 pounds or more, and this has become a yearly pilgrimage for some traveling kayak fly anglers. In the south, between Fort Lauderdale and Miami, you will find one of the feistiest fish that swims in freshwater. Originally from the South America, the peacock bass was introduced to help fight the spread of tilapia—another exotic species that was drastically affecting the native bass populations. These brightly colored fish have thrived in the area's extensive canal and lake systems and the kayak is the best way to fish for them as launch areas are sometimes located behind shopping centers or on roadside parks. Any lures that work for largemouth will work for peacocks. Remember, the hotter the weather, the hotter the fishing, so bring along plenty of water.

Although small, pound-for-pound, the Bonita puts up one of the best fights.

The Keys and Florida Bay

Everyone who fishes should spend some time in the Florida Keys. This chain of coral islands that stretch to the southwest from the Miami can offer fantastic sight-fishing for bonefish, tarpon, permit, jack crevalle, barracuda, sharks, redfish, and snook. One of the most fun and productive things to do is to sight-fish turtle grass flats. This is shallow-water fishing in depths as little as 6 inches for some of the most neurotic fish on the planet, so stealth is a non-negotiable and, luckily for us, there is nothing stealthier than a kayak. Even if you plan on only wade fishing, the mobility of a kayak will keep you in fish and provide you with a far greater variety of launch points than either a boat or purely fishing on foot. The experience of casting a fly to a tailing bonefish or rolling tarpon in gin-clear water while sitting in a kayak is something that can cause permanent heart murmurs, so best be ready for some excitement.

Florida Bay, which is the area between the tip of Florida and the Keys, is one of the most extensive and wild fisheries in the state. Without transporting your kayak by boat, the majority of

The Florida Keys offer endless kayak fishing opportunities.

the fishery is unreachable by the day paddler, but Everglades National Park, which can be accessed by car, offers access to the bay itself and the extensive backcountry around Whitewater Bay. One of the most unique kayak fishing experiences in the state can be had by loading up with camping gear and, from the put-in at Flamingo, paddling out to one of the many "chickees". A chickee is an elevated platform above the water featuring a slanted roof, port-a-john, and space for two tents. From this base camp, you can paddle to some of the wildest and most exciting fishing in the U.S. Tarpon, snook, redfish, jack crevalle, tripletail, and sharks are only some of the many species that are routinely encountered. For multi-day trips such as this, it pays to have a longer, higher-volume kayak that will allow you to travel quickly and carry a lot of gear. Keep in mind that there is no cell phone service here and very little boat traffic; a top quality first aid kit, tow belt, waterproof VHF radio, and extra food and water rations are only the beginning of a long list of safety gear that you should consider essential for such an adventure. Also know that it gets dark earlier in the Everglades than it does in the rest of Florida. This is not due to any astrological phenomenon, but rather the thick clouds of mosquitoes that appear at dusk. Can you say "DEET"?

Gulf Coast

The beaches of the Gulf Coast offer many of the same opportunities as the east coast with one primary difference—less surf. The gentler waters of the Gulf of Mexico make for great offshore kayak fishing for those less skilled in paddle and boat handling skills. In May, the beaches around Sanibel and Captiva Islands are usually teeming with tarpon. These fish, weighing up to 130 pounds, are easily accessed by kayak and sometimes the stealthier kayak anglers can out-fish those in boats. Throughout the summer, these same beaches offer excellent snook fishing in the mornings and evenings, as well as opportunities for other species throughout the year. Access from land can be difficult and a kayak cart is worth your loaded kayak's weight in gold.

While there is excellent beach fishing all the way up the Gulf Coast, another area that deserves mentioning is Sarasota. Known for its beautiful beaches and clear, blue waters, this more metropolitan fishery offers great beach fishing for tarpon, snook, Spanish mackerel, bonito, and kingfish just to name a few. There is also plenty of access to the water and many kayak-friendly parks to launch from.

Heading north to the mouth of Tampa Bay, Fort DeSoto Park is another kayak-friendly fishing destination.

There can be tremendous currents off the beach as water flows in and out of the bay, so monitor your tides and be conscious of changing conditions. The same fishing techniques employed on the east coast can reward you with tarpon, bonito, Spanish mackerel, kingfish, tripletail, sharks, and a host of other fishy targets.

The inshore fishing on the Gulf Coast is also very similar to that on the east coast in terms of species and fishing techniques. One main difference is the abundance of islands and extent of

A kayak cart can be invaluable on the Gulf Coast where access is limited.

backcountry. This is most evident in the south of Naples, appropriately named The Ten Thousand Islands. Chokoloskee is a good access point. GPS is definitely a good idea, as it is easy to get lost among the islands and creeks. This area blends into Everglades National Park as you head south; much of what you will read in the Florida Bay section of this article applies here.

Another geographic feature which defines the Gulf Coast is its systems of bays and sounds. In the more natural areas, you will find mud and grass flats and extensive mangrove shorelines broken up by tidal creeks and rivers. Pine Island Sound, near Fort Myers, is a top kayak fishing destination known for abundant but spooky redfish. Much of its waters are so shallow, especially in the winter months, that only kayaks can navigate easily. There is not a lot of access and a longer kayak will allow you to cover more water and make your experience much more productive. Seatrout and snook are also very common here and, depending on seasons, you may also run into tarpon, cobia, sharks, and more. Behind Pine Island is a little town called Matlacha. It is a favored area for many traveling kayak anglers, as there is very easy access from the many inexpensive waterfront accommodations, not to mention a few great restaurants and bars that are accessible by kayak.

Other inshore areas that have a following among kayak anglers are Sarasota Bay, Tampa Bay, Homosassa, Crystal River, and The Cedar Keys. Important considerations when kayak fishing inshore waters on the Gulf Coast are the shallowness of the fishery is and the sight-fishing, which can be far more productive than blind casting. Sometimes, to get to the fish, you must travel in water that is too shallow for your paddle blade. Push poles and stake out poles are common here and foot-operated rudders are becoming more prevalent. With a 5- to 6-foot push pole and rudder, you can pole up to a tailing redfish while staying seated and anchor the kayak with the pole. This offers a stealthier approach, where you don't have to take your eyes off of the fish.

Freshwater fishing on the west coast of Florida can be a relative term. It is not uncommon to be bass fishing and hook a small tarpon or snook, even many miles from the coast. Case in point is the Big Cypress National Preserve, east of Naples. This huge park not only teems with big gators, but also a wide variety of fresh and saltwater game fish, not to mention a myriad of exotic species like oscars, Mayan cichlids, and tilapia. There are several areas from which to launch a kayak and ample camping, but it is wise to purchase both fresh and saltwater fishing licenses rather than worry about where exactly you are fishing.

Scott Null just outside the Everglades National Park.

Panhandle

Kayak fishing opportunities in the Panhandle vary from pursuing redfish, seatrout, and flounder in salt marsh bays, to hunting bigger game like cobia, tarpon, and big bull redfish slightly offshore. Fishing offshore in the Panhandle involves deeper water than the southern Gulf Coast, and getting into pelagic fish like dolphin, billfish, kingfish, and the like could be possible out of the kayak by mothershipping farther out. Launching from shore and pursuing large pods of bait can get you into bull reds, mackerel, and ladyfish, just to mention a few. The Panhandle has many large bay systems, which feature everything from open water to salt marshes, to mud flats and oyster bars. Fishing these inshore waters with flies, plugs, soft plastics and live baits can all be productive. Whether inshore or offshore, the major cities in this part of the state all offer great opportunities and major bays like St. Andrew Bay in Panama City, Choctawhatchee Bay in Destin, and Pensacola Bay in Pensacola are all excellent places to wet both a paddle and a line. Whether you are a Floridian new to kayak fishing or a kayak angler planning a vacation somewhere in the state, understanding the basic geography of the area, local fishing techniques, and what tackle to use, as well as having the appropriately rigged kayak and safety equipment could make all the difference in terms of the fun you will have and the fish you will catch. Spending some time researching up-to-date local fishing reports and examining the area on Google Earth is always a good idea, and time spent with a local guide is absolutely invaluable. It is also a good idea to patronize the local tackle and kayak shops; they want you to have a fun and productive time on the water every bit as much as you do. And don't forget to bring along a camera. Manatees, dolphins, raccoons, otters, and countless species of birds are common sights during a day of paddling in many of Florida's great fisheries.

Joel McBride works the mangroves just outside Chokoloskee.

Kayak Fishing Texas

By Scott Null

I've lived in Texas my entire life and I've fished all over the state for more than 40 years. I've targeted everything from blue water predators in the open Gulf to sunfish at the local park. With over 6,700 square miles of water, the variety and diversity of fishing in this state could warrant an entire book. Texas' Gulf Coast, 367 miles long from Louisiana to Mexico, includes over 600 miles of tidewater coastline and hundreds of square miles of open bay and tidal marshes. Add to that nearly 6,800 named lakes, 3,700 named streams, 15 major rivers, and untold farm ponds. Within these waters resides a staggering diversity of fish. The Texas Parks and Wildlife Department maintains record catches for over 200 species in saltwater and 87 species in freshwater, including 12 species of bass. If a Texan ever says he can't find a place to fish, he just isn't trying hard enough.

Access to all of these waters has increased dramatically over the last few years with the growing popularity of kayak fishing. Even the angler on a tight budget can get set up with a kayak and begin exploring new water for a fraction of the cost of owning and operating a powerboat. As you become more experienced and confident, there are very few places or species in Texas that you can't target from a kayak. Given good weather and calm conditions, I'll fish from a kayak just about anywhere I'd fish in a powerboat.

The winding mangrove channels around Matagorda Island.

Coastal Inshore Waters

Beginning kayakers would do well to stick to the shallow protected marshes, coves and flats of the bay. All along the Texas coast, redfish, speckled trout and flounder are the primary targets; the kayak is the perfect tool for making a quiet approach and catching undisturbed fish. And in South Texas you might even find a snook, as they appear to be making a strong showing with the recent mild winters.

Feeding fish are often visible in this environment. By paddling slowly and remaining alert you'll often see baitfish fleeing from predators. In the case of redfish, you can sometimes spot them either tailing or cruising with their backs exposed in just a few inches of water. Tailing fish are rooting the bottom in search of shrimp or crabs. These fish are often so distracted that a kayaker can approach very close without spooking them. Simply toss an imitation shrimp such as a DOA in front of them and you'll get some action.

At certain times of the year, gulls and terns will gather over open water in bays and lakes to feast on baitfish being pushed to the surface by schools of fish. There are few things more exciting than paddling into a frenzy of feeding fish.

Trout are typically a schooling fish, but trophy loners are often found in the same shallow waters where redfish feed. And flounder can be targeted from a kayak by exploring the mouths of marsh drains or any place with a pronounced current. They are ambush feeders, lying in wait on the bottom for a baitfish or shrimp to be carried past by moving water.

Lakes and Ponds

Freshwater anglers will find that a kayak is a great tool for getting way back into thick cover in search of bass and crappie. Inexperienced kayakers can feel comfortable fishing these areas away from the boat traffic of the open lake; most of the time you'll be fairly close to the bank. Many of these places never see an angler because a boat can't squeeze in there. Vertically jigging in the thickest cover is a good way to pull out a big bass. Just be aware of the barely submerged tree tops on the larger reservoirs, as unexpectedly paddling over them can cause you to overturn. You can also explore the bounty of deeper structure by adding a depth finder to your kayak.

Rivers and Streams

Once you get comfortable with your abilities, a trip down a moving river can put you into some great untapped fishing. The Hill Country of Central Texas is full of beautiful rocky streams and rivers that aren't navigable by boat. The areas just

below rapids and the deeper pools hold a surprising number of bass, including the scrappy native Guadalupe bass and several species of sunfish.

With some experience, you can navigate a fishing kayak through most any rapid you are likely to encounter in Texas (under normal flow conditions), but there is certainly no shame in portaging around a dicey situation. Guidebooks for floating most of the major waterways are available and you can obtain flow rates and conditions via the Internet or local outdoor shops.

The Surf Zone and Offshore Waters

Along the beachfront, you can launch from the sand and fish just past the breakers for surf-run speckled trout, Spanish mackerel, and big mature redfish or sharks. Whether you're soaking bait or chunking lures, the surf zone can produce throughout the year.

For the most experienced kayakers, there is the open water of the Gulf, where you can tangle with king mackerel, cobia, red snapper and other hard-pulling pelagic species throughout the summer and early fall. These trips are not to be taken lightly, as paddling several miles offshore can be extremely dangerous. Big fish and changing weather conditions can turn a fun day of fishing into a dire situation very quickly. Plan accordingly, watch the weather and surround yourself with as many experienced kayak anglers as possible when venturing out to the blue water. On the right days, these can be extremely rewarding trips. You are pitting yourself against the hardest-pulling fish, in a challenging environment, from a craft most anglers would never even consider capable of such duty.

Resources

As to where to go, any public place where you can safely park and launch is fair game. I rely heavily on Google Earth. Anytime I'm driving, I'm looking for possible launches. Some of my favorite fishing places have been discovered when I crossed a bridge over a small bayou or even a ditch. Later, a quick search on the computer will tell me where that waterway leads. Along the coast, you'll often find that the bayou leads to some secluded marsh that gets very little, if any pressure. In other parts of the state, a small stream will often feed into a cove on a lake that can't easily be

accessed any other way. Or it joins with a larger river where private property along the banks restricts access. Use your imagination and you'll be surprised at how many fishing opportunities there are for a kayak angler.

In addition to the readily available fishing maps, another indispensable tool for anglers is an aerial map. At many local tackle shops, you can find laminated aerial photo maps for most every area along the coast, and many of the major lakes. These are small enough to keep with you in the kayak and come in handy when exploring new water. If you study the maps and spend some time on the water, you can begin to get a feel for the way the water flows through the marshes and around reefs or other structure. Locating these areas within your fishing grounds is more than half the battle in becoming a successful fisherman.

Unfortunately many miles of shoreline surrounding our Texas bays is private property. But there are many options available for launching a kayak. A good friend of mine, Ray Crawford, has done extensive research and driven hundreds of miles searching out these hidden jewels. Ray has chosen to share these spots in the form of two guidebooks titled *Wade and Kayak Fishing Galveston Bay*, covering much of the Upper Coast, and *Wade and Kayak Fishing on the Coastal Bend of Texas*, covering the Middle Coast. These books include aerial photos, maps, and driving directions, as well as tips to effectively fishing the different areas. The Middle Coast book alone has over 300 places to legally park and launch. Every coastal angler should have these books in their library. My tattered copies ride in the truck with me.

Another great source for information on anything related to kayak fishing in Texas is the website www.texaskayakfisherman.com. Whether you are looking for information on a particular area, or a buddy to go fishing with, this site has it all.

To sum it up, Texas has virtually unlimited opportunity for the kayak angler. You just have to get out there and make it happen.

California Dreamin': Exploring the Golden State's Spectacular Kayak Fishing

By Paul Lebowitz

Kayak fishing the Golden State is an oh-dark-thirty beach launch culminating in a dance with fork-tailed lightning, the turbo charged California yellowtail.

It's sneaking up on that most skittish of king croakers, the grey ghosts of the kelp beds, the mysterious white seabass. It's close-quarters battle with California halibut, the tasty flatfish that love to play possum until they're in your lap.

California kayak fishing is chasing saltwater bass in the Southland's bays, willing fighters that keep a pole bent all day. Their bigger cousins, the calicos, wait outside, deep in the thickest, boat-hating weeds or danger-close to wave-swept rocks.

Up north, the saltwater scene is a hunt for sea monsters; sharp-fanged, blue-fleshed lingcod and massive, primeval sturgeon. Or it's a near-guarantee of that fish 'n' chips staple, rock cod, wearing every color of the rainbow on their hides and flaky white flesh on the inside.

All this and more, California kayak fishing is a vast banquet of mild to wild experiences. Here's a closer look at the sport's West Coast hotbed.

Josh Rider with a halibut around San Clemente.
PHOTO BY PAUL LEBOWITZ

Mark Pierpont with a calico bass.
PHOTO BY PAUL LEBOWITZ

Southern California's Bountiful Ocean

The most southerly stretch of the state offers up the hottest kayak fishing—literally. Warmer water means this is the place to tangle with active fish such as yellowtail, sleek kayak-towing jacks averaging 15 to 20 pounds. They are always in residence at La Jolla, the epicenter California kayak fishing. White seabass are another regular visitor. These croakers reach upwards of 60 pounds, yet are super shy. Boats scare them; not so the stealthy kayak. Both of these prime targets will snap up a live mackerel presented on the slow troll or the drift, or chomp on a deftly worked iron. Pack the big guns; conventional saltwater gear spooled up with 20- to 30-pound string.

Kelp bass play here too. They are a Southern Californian's most dependable ocean adversary. Commonly known as calicos for their checkered coats, these aggressive fish love to hunker down in dense kelp forests and jagged reefs. The real trophies camp out on surf-washed rocks, another perilous place for powerboats. Daring kayakers can go right in there to get them. Calicos eat just about any artificial bait between 3 and 7 inches long, from topwater slugs to bottom-scratching jigs. Find them at their densest from glitzy Malibu south to sunny San Diego.

Spring and fall are the top months for California halibut. When the powerful ambush predators flow into the shallow water just outside the surf zone to spawn, they are pretty much in a kayak angler's exclusive fishing hole. Get them by slowly bouncing live baits along sandy bottoms.

Other species migrate in seasonally, following warm pulses of bait-rich water. Barracuda and bonito flurries ignite inshore action from spring through fall. Thresher sharks thunder in from time to time, pushing even experts to the edge.

Southern California's bays and harbors offer up excellent kayak fishing. Calm, easy-launch waters such as San Diego, Mission, and Newport are ideal for those first casts. They are home to a pugnacious little bay bass, the spotty. There are halibut too, even big ones, plus sand bass, barracuda, bonito, and even the odd surprise such as the bonefish, which scoot around in south San Diego Bay. Feed any of these fish small plastic grubs, swimbaits and cranks on 6- to 15-pound line.

Southern California's Coastal Crown Jewels: La Jolla; Dana Point; San Pedro's Cabrillo Beach; Redondo / King Harbor; star-studded Malibu; Two Harbors, Catalina; and San Clemente Island via mothership.

The Rugged North

North of Point Conception, the Pacific Ocean rarely lives up to its name. This is a challenging place, where the water is usually frigid and frequently rough. The tough conditions and a shortage of sheltered launch sites keep all but the hardiest adventurers off the water.

Ah, but there are great rewards for those who dare the mighty surf. Rockfish are the chief bread and butter; in remoter areas, it is difficult to get a bait down deep to the bigger bottom dwellers. Smaller fish smack it at the surface.

The lingcod is top of the heap here. A ferociously aggressive predator, lingcod look like something from another planet, with huge, snaggle-toothed smiles, sinewy bodies, and—no kidding—flesh of a sickly green or blue tinge (note to the squeamish: delicious lingcod cook to a flaky, ivory white).

Lingcod and rockfish fall for the same tricks: 4- to 7-inch twin-tail or grub-tail plastics; irons and metal jigs danced vertically; and natural baits such as cut squid. Salmon are a rare but highly esteemed kayak catch in the northern reaches of California. When the season is open, kayakers watch carefully until vast bait schools move in tight to the coast. Then they pounce, trolling or mooching dead fin baits.

Then there are the dinosaurs, fish

A rough landing on the rugged north coast. PHOTO BY PAUL LEBOWITZ

of the frozen fingers. During the rainy season, kayak anglers with antifreeze for blood anchor up in the powerful and hazardous currents of greater San Francisco Bay and other brackish waters, enticing huge, hundred-plus-pound sturgeon with tiny shrimp. The bay and delta also host another great kayak game fish, an East Coast import and pinstriped torpedo known more commonly as the striped bass.

Northern California's Special Salty Places: Stillwater Cove, Morro Bay; lower Big Sur; Monterey and Carmel; Santa Cruz; Pigeon Point; Fort Ross; and various non-sharky spots farther north. Although more of a menace to the imagination than a threat to life and limb, great white sharks are common around the area's marine mammal colonies, so avoid these areas.

Getting Fresh

Most of California's kayak fishing scene plays out on saltwater, but the sweet stuff has its place. The Golden State builds big largemouth bass, the heaviest in the country. The fishing world's most storied record could legitimately fall to a sneaky-stealthy kayaker.

The state's skyscraping spine, the Sierras and other jagged peaks, hide small, crystalline mountain lakes in their folds. The home of several species of wild and native trout, these high altitude waters are prime kayak fishing country.

Intrepid northerners are pioneering another kayak fishery, pristine and otherwise unreachable steelhead streams. They hop out and work likely holes from the bank, or risk anchoring and fish right from their rides.

California's Slick Sleds

The modern, self-draining, sit-on-top fishing kayak was born on California's shores, the brainchild of Malibu's Tim Niemier. Since he cooked up his first Scupper, the form has advanced incrementally to its current sophistication. Everything has its place on the newest crop of kayaks, and that's great, 'cause California kayak anglers rig their rides to the hilt.

It's the rare California fishing kayak that doesn't sport fancy electronics. Fish finders are valuable tools for most of the state's fisheries. Bass hunters and rock cod rippers alike rely on them to identify fish-holding structure. And then there's bait location, a mission-critical task down south, where live mackerel are the key to most big-game ocean catches.

The dual purpose live well and bait tank is the next staple gizmo, indispensable in the live-bait ocean fisheries down south. It is a must-have for bass tournament battlers who want to keep their fish kicking until their big-league-style weigh-ins.

Otherwise, California kayak anglers rig their rides much the same as their cousins across the country, although perhaps with an extra rod holder or two. Due to the diversity of the local fisheries, it's quite common to tote four or five rods strung up and ready to rock at a moment's notice.

The surf is always a consideration. Kayak anglers who challenge the big stuff—breakers up to 5 feet or so—need boats that strip down to a clean deck. Where crash landings are common, belowdeck storage is a must.

Because California kayak anglers often find themselves out in open water miles from their launch sites, safety gear is a wise investment. Most carry submersible handheld marine VHF radios. Ostensibly for calling the Coast Guard when the chips are down, they are terrific for communicating with fishing buddies. Other gear commonly packed includes: a kayak pump, drift and kelp anchors, a handheld GPS, a compass, extra clothes in a dry bag, a first aid kit, and sometimes, an EPIRB and flares.

A Lifetime's Worth of Kayak Fishing Water

As you've seen, kayak fishing opportunities abound in California, where the sport has definitely hit the mainstream. The colorful plastic boats are a common sight at fishing holes across the vast state. Kayak fishing's tremendous popularity continues to open new avenues of adventure, such as mothership trips to the remote Channel Islands. These spectacular specks of land can only be reached with motorized assistance, but once there, kayaks get anglers into the nooks and crannies, where fish have never seen a hook.

The best is yet to come. Come cast a line in California, kayak fishing's Golden State.

Kayak Fishing East Coast Style

By Kevin Whitley

When thinking of the East Coast, one might envision a sprawling metropolitan cityscape, busy with commercial ship traffic, unfriendly to the kayak angler. Although the coast is dotted with highly industrial and populated areas, the reality is the Eastern Seaboard is as wild and burly as when Captain John Smith landed on Cape Henry at the mouth of the Chesapeake Bay in 1607.

Kayak fishing really started to take off on the East Coast around 2004 and has grown incredibly in the years since, as more and more anglers realize they can catch more fish from kayaks. It basically started with shore-bound anglers finding a cheaper way to get off the

Kevin with a big red on the Virginia shoals.

beach. Now, boat-owning anglers are getting into the game for the ease and convenience of inshore inlet fishing.

The universal advantage of kayak fishing the East Coast is being able to get into shallow creeks and flats that boats can't, or getting there first. When the stripers and bluefish blitz erupts at dawn off the beach, a kayaker can punch through the surf after them before the boats have even left the docks. As the sport has grown, kayak anglers have learned to target everything within a 3- to 4-mile range from the launch. I asked top kayak anglers from the Northeast, North Carolina, and Georgia about the targets, techniques, and challenges of fishing their region.

Northeast

Al Stillman is the founder of eastcoastkayakfishing.com and a member of the Hobie Kayak Fishing Team. The ECKF website is the go-to site in his stomping ground of the Jersey and New York coasts.

In mid-April, Al starts out fishing for striped bass in the bays and back rivers, heading to places like New Jersey's Raritan Bay, near Sandy Hook, and Jamaica Bay, New York. He drifts or anchors with clams on fish-finder rigs.

"As the bays warm, finding huge pods of bunker and snagging them to live-line them has to be one of the most exciting ways to catch huge stripers," Al says. He trolls and casts into diving birds with bucktails and metal for the best results. "As the water warms in June, the bunker move out front off the beaches and you now need to have your act together to launch and land from the beaches." He reports pulling 60-pound stripers off the beaches.

Bunker is the main bait in his area for big fish. "When I approach a school with a kayak," says Al, "they are usually so thick that you can feel them hitting the bottom of your kayak. A short cast with the bunker snagger and you're off to landing the big one and screaming reels."

Come September, Al heads to Montauk, New York. Montauk Point is the toughest place he fishes. Big stripers and false albacore congregate around this famous rocky point. "This area can be a very rewarding place if you can catch the weather right. The wind and the tide are a factor almost every time out."

Kevin with a sheepshead.

Georgia

The Georgia coast is as raw and burly a place as you can get. I paddled through it on two different tours and the region is definitely the most challenging on the East Coast. Redfish, flounder, speckled trout, and sheepshead are plentiful and roam the vast, winding marshes. Although the Georgia coastline is an intimidating place, kayak anglers have found their way there.

One of the biggest challenges in Georgia is the big tides and swift current. Georgia sits way in on the continental shelf. The shape of the eastern shoreline funnels the sea into what is known as the Georgia Bight. This funnel stacks the water on top of itself, creating the giant tide. Locals plan their fishing trips to run in and out with the tide. "You can anchor or stake out once you reach a spot, but getting back can be very difficult if the current is running too strongly," says angler Mike Sueirro. "I often find myself choosing a fishing location based on the currents. I paddle or drift with the current to the spot and when the tide reverses, follow it back to the launch."

During the spring tides around the full and new moon the tidal range can be 8 to 10 feet, muddying the water and making it nearly impossible to fish.

To find the specks, Georgia kayak anglers look for clean moving water close to shell mounds and grassy points. Reds can be found around the same structures and downed trees. Reds will also hunt the flats on an incoming tide to root out crabs, snails, and shrimp. Flounder will wait to ambush bait at the mouths of creeks and channel edges. Sheepshead pick crustaceans on any structure.

"For trout, a shrimp or mud-minnow under a float for live bait and the DOA soft plastic paddle tails on a jig head fished around grass or shells are productive," explains local angler Mark Mund. "Reds will eat just about anything, but when they are keyed to feeding on one thing, it's hard to get them to bite anything else. A soft plastic on a jig head or better yet a Gulp! fished on or near the bottom is good. They will hit topwater plugs when they are feeding on shallow flats, chasing mullet. The saltwater spinnerbaits are also deadly on reds fished in and around grass and structure. For flounder, a soft plastic or Gulp! on a jig head, or the saltwater spinnerbaits are good when fished slow around creek mouths and drop-offs. They also love a mud-minnow dragged slowly across the bottom. Sheepshead are best caught right up against structure with either a fiddler crab or a shrimp. Some people use oysters or mussels for bait also."

A 52-pound striper.

North Carolina

Ryan Hunnicutt started kayak fishing about five years ago, after moving to Wilmington, North Carolina. His fishing grounds are the waters in and around the Cape Fear region. The big three species targeted inshore are red drum, specked trout and flounder.

"All three species can be caught anywhere from the tidal creeks and protected bays to the Cape Fear River, Intracoastal Waterway, inlets, and surf," says Ryan. "We also target sheepshead along inshore structure such as docks, bridges, and oyster bars. Black drum can be found in most of these same locations as well. In the spring we get

a pretty good run of 6- to 15-pound chopper blues, which can be found in all the same areas as drum, trout, and flounder. They simply follow the bait."

"Reds can be caught in a large variety of ways. Natural bait is usually a sure thing to get them to eat, but I normally prefer to target them from the kayak with artificial lures in shallow water.

Mike Basnite lands a monster black drum.

Besides, it's just more fun, challenging, and rewarding. When it comes to targeting them on lures, it's a lot like bass fishing. Any lure that resembles a small baitfish, shrimp, or crab can generally produce strikes. Popular lures include soft plastics on jig heads or weighted hooks, spinnerbaits, suspending hard baits, topwater plugs and plastic shrimp imitations. Many bass lures such as plastic worms, jigs, and tubes can work great on reds as well. Generally, I like to go with the lightest-weight jig or hook that I can get away with based on the conditions. Trout will hit most of the same baits and lures as reds. Typically, but not always, they like to hang out in a little deeper water."

Ryan also tackles king mackerel and cobia off of the beach, "Launching through the surf and fishing the ocean is about as burly as we normally get around here. It can get a little interesting on the nasty days, but we try our best to avoid those."

Cobias make their appearance to the lower Carolina coast in May through June. "With live baits on the surface, I can basically fish for both kings and cobia at the same time during the spring run, when both species are on the beach. I also like to anchor near structure and fish live baits on the bottom when specifically targeting cobia. One of the challenges when targeting them in the kayak is actually catching the bait. Without a live well, it's hard to catch bait ahead of time. I keep my baits in a small, flow-troll type bucket while on the water. Some days, bait is very easy to catch and this is a non-issue, but many days, you end up spending a lot of fishing time just trying to catch anything worth using. When you finally do get decent bait, sharks can invade and it's back to square one."

With heavy summer boat traffic in the Cape Fear area, Ryan recommends fishing mid-week, as well as at sunrise and sunset when the fishing is better anyway.

Ryan says that inshore and backwater fishing has had a new life with kayakers stealthily stalking the shallows. "Not only does a kayak lack a noisy motor to spook fish, but its small size makes it easy to pole/maneuver and creates less of a pressure wave than a larger boat. In shallow water, this can be the difference between catching and not catching. It's a lot easier to catch a relaxed, happy fish than a stressed out fish that senses danger."

Virginia

With all of the incredible fishing on the East Coast, I'm lucky enough to live smack dab in the middle of it. My fishing grounds are the lower Chesapeake Bay. The bay is the northernmost migration point for the southern fish and the

If you travel into unsheltered waters on the east coast, large waves can drum up quickly.

southernmost point of the northern fish. The Chesapeake attracts everything from stripers to tarpon.

The Chesapeake's inlets, rivers, and bridges are full of species like small striper, red drum, speckled trout, flounder, bluefish, croaker, and the small but tasty spot. All of these fisheries are accessible for after-work fishing sessions with ease in a kayak. My favorite fish to target are the big and hard-to-get fish. This starts in April, when we cast whole crabs into big rolling ocean breakers for big bull red drum.

Virginia trophy red drum start at 46 inches. Reds in the 50-inch range are not uncommon. The shoals on the Virginia Eastern Shore are the burliest place we fish. The breakers can be big and the fish are tough. It's not uncommon to anchor off in 5 to 6 knots of current and 5-foot breakers—and then hook up to a big red!

The next big fish to migrate into the 3- to 4-mile paddling range is the cobia. The main tactic is anchoring on the inner bay shoals and soaking cut baits in a chum slick. But cobia could be spotted anywhere in the bay, so I always have a cobia lure ready when I'm paddling in the summer.

In the summer months, I spend most of my time at the longest man-made reef in the world. The Chesapeake Bay Bridge-Tunnel (CBBT) is a 16-mile span across the mouth of the Chesapeake.

The four rock islands that make the entrances to the two channel tunnels have so many fish around them that it's hard to fully target them all in a day. Doormat-size flounder wait in ambush mode in the rocks. I pull them out with 2-ounce jig heads and a large Gulp! Huge black drum from 50 to 90 pounds circle around the islands. I sight-cast to these monsters with a 1-ounce jig head and the same Gulp!.

The main targets of the islands are toutog, triggerfish, and sheepshead. These three make up the island slam. The CBBT has some of the biggest sheepshead anywhere. The Virginia state record is 20 pounds, 12 ounces—just 8 ounces under the world record. The island fish are caught using cut blue, fiddler, and hermit crab.

One distinct advantage of targeting the island in a kayak is the maneuverability around the pilings and the rocks. I set right up against the pilings of the bridge, actually rubbing and bumping against them on every wave. You can't do that in a boat without causing a thousand dollars' worth of damage.

In the winter, the Chesapeake becomes the striper capital of the world. The entire migratory population enters the bay. For kayak striper chasers, the concrete ships off of Kiptopeke on the Virginia Eastern Shore are the easiest place in the world to land trophy stripers. The ships are WWII cargo ships made out of rebar and concrete. Nine of them were sunk 200 yards offshore as a breakwater for the ferry that ran before the CBBT was built. They are a formidable structure and a big striper attractant. Not only is it a short paddle in protected water, the technique is super simple. Live eels on a 9/0 j-hook with a 2-once egg sinker, suspended 2 to 3 feet off the bottom, is all it takes. I use one rod with the reel in free spool and the clicker on. I sit on the rod butt and hover against the concrete wall with my paddle. Too close for boats, this is a kayak-only technique.

The bay tides are only half as big as Georgia's, but in some places it can rip at 6 knots. Like everywhere else on the East Coast, sudden storms can pop up in the summer months causing a deadly situation. Fast-moving currents and rapidly developing storms can turn a nice day on the water in a small plastic boat into a hazardous situation. I consider a VHF radio a mandatory piece of safety equipment. The NOAA weather reports will warn of a storm before you can see it through the summer haze.

East Coast fishing is beautifully burly and offers a plentiful variety of fish. Kayak anglers have learned and developed techniques to catch anything and everything that comes into paddling range.

The rugged Alaskan coast.

Kayak Fishing Alaska Style

By Howard McKim

Alaska. The mere word conjures up grand images in most of our minds. Wild. Vast. Extreme. Unforgiving. All certainly true, but what does it mean to the kayak angler? Alaska was the birthplace of kayak fishing, and it was proven long ago that the kayak and Alaskan water are an excellent match. It was here that the art of kayak fishing took root, and though the kayak plays a less critical role today, it remains an effective tool for both harvest and recreation.

The Alexander Archipelago of Southeast Alaska, or simply "Southeast" as it is called, offers over 11,000 miles of coastline, perfectly fit for a kayak and an adventurous spirit. There are a seemingly endless number of small islands and protected waterways that would take more than a lifetime to explore. It is a place where dense rainforest meets the sea along rugged coastlines that stretch as far as the imagination. Steep mountains rise straight up from the sea, with snowcapped peaks breaking up the often cloudy skies. Rain falls heavy. Tides swing quickly. Life abounds.

Few places offer the kayak angler such vast opportunities. Here, the conscientious paddler can take to the sea, catch dinner, land on an island, make a fire, and cook a seafood feast that will be etched into permanent memory. You can paddle day after day, providing for yourself along the way, without ever seeing another person. This is public land. No permits or permissions are required.

The Tongass National Forest stretches over 17 million acres of Southeast and has very few towns or roads. Self reliance is paramount, as help is often nowhere near. Alaska has a way of distracting you, and any weakness in mind, body, or equipment will be exploited. It is important to carry basic survival gear,

The fishing was so good on this day that Howard catches a rockfish using beer caps as a lure.

and more important to know how to use it. A small dry bag with radio, bivy, fire starters, and a simple cook set can ease the mind when conditions on the water worsen. Despite the challenges, the kayak angler with an eye on the horizon will be filled with a spirit of adventure that is quickly fading in the chaos of modern times.

Cold, nutrient-rich waters provide a wealth of resources for the kayak angler. All five types of Pacific salmon and a huge array of bottom fish frequent the Inside Passage. Salmon come in waves throughout the summer months, starting with king salmon in June. These run through mid-July and are soon followed by the pink and chum, and finally the coho toward the end of summer. Sockeye are rarely caught with rod and reel, as they feed mostly on plankton and other invertebrates.

Although it's tough to beat a nice, shiny salmon caught from the kayak, bottom fishing in Alaska is second to none. One of the distinct features of kayak fishing Alaska is that you never know what you'll catch when you drop to the bottom. Though you may target a particular species, just about anything can end up on your line. A 2-pound rockfish or a 200-pound halibut could be eyeing the bait. It is not uncommon to catch rockfish, lingcod, and halibut all in the same area. This makes equipment choices a bit difficult. Kayak fishing techniques are quite different than what local boaters use. Drift fishing from a kayak is very effective, and with tide swings up to 22 feet, there is no shortage of current to pull you along. Typical fishing depths are 150 to 300 feet, using weight up to 8 ounces. Fast-sinking lures are preferable; these are bounced off the bottom as the current drifts the kayak over large areas of water.

The idea is to go find the fish instead of anchoring and waiting for something to come to you. Make a grid pattern with your drifts and you'll know you covered the area well.

For salmon, both trolling and mooching are used. Trolling is more productive in late summer for pink and coho salmon, as these are closer to the surface and not quite as finicky as king salmon. Herring and a variety of lures are all effective and can be trolled with minimal weight. Drop the line, position the rod, and just paddle around in the infinite beauty surrounding you. It's easy to forget you're even fishing, until your kayak starts pulling backward.

For mooching rigs, two 3/0 to 5/0 octopus hooks are snell tied about 5 inches apart. Cut plug or whole herring

The typical halibut going nuts alongside the kayak.

are hooked in a fashion so that the bait spins as it goes through the water, and 2 feet above the hooks is a 2- to 4-ounce banana weight. Drop this down to the desired depth and work it back up to the kayak using long, broad strokes with the rod, Each time the rod tip is lowered the slack line should be brought in. This is done on the drift like bottom fishing, and unlike trolling you can cover all depths with each drop. Be sure to look behind the bait before you pull it out of the water; often a salmon is cruising right behind it.

Fish are not the only things a kayaker can get from the sea. Huge prawns and stout dungeness crabs can be taken with minimal gear. Pots are used for both of these, and with a little effort it's sometimes stunning to see the results. Shrimp pots are typically set 300 feet or deeper, and the crab are usually 100 feet or less. The pots are left overnight, and it's good to check them daily. Saved carcasses from filleted fish make excellent bait. Recycling at its finest.

Kayak fishing in Alaska encompasses far more than just catching fish from a kayak. It's about wide open spaces, where the angler can connect with his environment without distraction. It's about self sufficiency and using your head. It's about the unknown. If you're after a kayak fishing experience beyond the typical, come and drop a line into the depths of The Last Frontier.

CHAPTER 8

kayak fishing safety

PHOTO BY LISA OXLEY

WITH A LITTLE CARE and common sense, kayak fishing is a very safe sport that can be enjoyed by people of all ages. However, because you do it out on the water, it can get quite serious fast if things go wrong. It's for this reason that it is important that you understand and appreciate the risks and hazards involved with kayak fishing. You must assume a conservative and safety-conscious attitude when making decisions on the water.

Avoiding dangerous situations on the water is surprisingly easy. First and foremost, understand that alcohol and boating simply don't go together. Regrettably, alcohol is a major factor in nearly all boating accidents. It's also critical that you wear a PFD whenever you're on the water. By investing in a kayak fishing-specific PFD that is designed to be as comfortable and unrestricting as possible, you'll eliminate virtually any reason for wanting to remove it. These PFDs also effectively replace fishing vests. In the warmer climates, where the water you'll be fishing is no more that knee deep, there's a tendency to not wear a PFD. Invariably though, an angler thinks, "Hey, maybe it'll be better over on the other side of the channel." Next thing you know, they are paddling across deep water without their lifejacket, but dealing with powerboats and their wakes. Make it part of your put-in ritual. Got my lures, check, got water, check, wearing my PFD, check! It's simple, and it could save your life.

On a similar note, you need to dress for the conditions. Cold water represents the biggest hazard, because being immersed in cold water can result in hypothermia very quickly. If you're paddling in cold water, you need to be even more conservative in your decisions. Paddle only in calm conditions, stay close to shore, never paddle alone, and keep in mind that you're better off overdressing and being too warm than being too cold. With all that cold water around, it's easy to cool yourself off! And cooling off when you're hot is always easier than warming up when you're cold.

Another important safety issue to address is how to deal with boat traffic. It's important to know the rules of the road—or the water. Know that when you are crossing a channel in traffic, or when you are approaching an inlet, you should yield to oncoming traffic. Your biggest concern should be the powerboats and personal watercraft that can zip around the water erratically. The best way to avoid them is to stay close to shore. It's also smart to wear a brightly colored PFD and clothing to help make you more visible. Whatever the situation, remember that you are in a kayak and, just like you wouldn't bring a knife to a gunfight, don't think you can successfully challenge a powerboater or expect them to back down. Use discretion and live to paddle and fish another day.

Dealing with Weather

Weather will always have a bearing on whether or not you should go kayak fishing, and depending on where you're paddling, you'll have different weather hazards to deal with.

In large bodies of water and on the ocean, the biggest weather concerns are wind and waves. Strong winds can push you around and make it impossible to move forward. Gusts of wind can even catch you off-guard and flip you over. Furthermore, wind can drum up waves surprisingly quickly, which only further complicates things. Avoid getting caught in nasty, windy and rough conditions. If you're going to be heading onto a big body of water, check the weather report beforehand and stay close to shore if there is any doubt regarding the conditions.

Fog can also be a serious problem. In many areas, fog is quite common and can roll in quickly. The key to paddling in fog, or in areas that are subject to having fog roll in, is to hug the shoreline. You can then just turn around and follow the same shoreline back home. As a bonus, sticking close to shore pretty much guarantees you'll be out of the way of motorized boat traffic.

Rain on its own is no big deal when you're out in a kayak. In fact, paddling in the rain can be a really cool experience. But the unfortunate truth is that rain is usually accompanied by other weather. You know how to deal with wind, but what about thunder and lightning? If you hear thunder, then you know that there's lightning around, which is very dangerous to anyone out on the water. When on the water, you're usually the highest point for quite a distance in any direction, making you a perfect lightning rod. At the first hint of thunder or lightning, get off the water immediately and wait until the storm passes by.

Fog can be a serious problem on open water. It's amazing how quickly you can become disoriented. If you plan on paddling on open water where fog is common, make sure you have a compass, map and/or GPS.

Choosing a Safe Fishing Location

One of the easiest ways to stay safe and ensure that your kayak fishing experience is fun for everyone is to choose an appropriate fishing spot. Most importantly, unless you are experienced and equipped to deal with exposed conditions, you'll want to pick a fishing location that's sheltered from both wind and waves. Although the ocean and large lakes can sometimes be incredibly calm and provide an ideal kayak fishing environment, it's important to recognize that conditions can quickly change.

If you choose to paddle in exposed areas, where conditions can deteriorate really quickly, you should always check the weather forecast before heading out, and keep your eyes open for signs of bad weather moving in while you're paddling, whether it's forecasted or not. Also, make sure that you know of a variety of different take out points so that you won't feel compelled to challenge the elements just to get back to the one place you know you can get out.

The ideal kayaking environment has a good access point for launching, lots of places to easily go ashore and minimal motorized on-water traffic. Look for calm bays or quiet lakes and riverways. Although it can be tempting to search out the most remote location possible, bear in mind that if you ever did need a little assistance, it's awfully nice to know there will be someone around who can lend a hand.

Kayak Fishing Alone

Of course, every situation is unique; when deciding whether or not it's a good idea to go fishing alone, common sense should prevail. If you're simply heading out onto a local pond to do some bass fishing, or fishing some protected, knee-deep flats, then fishing alone isn't a big deal. If you're going to be straying into deeper, colder, and/or less-sheltered water, targeting larger fish, or traveling further from shore than you can easily swim, then as a general rule, kayak fishing alone is a bad idea for the simple reason that when things do go wrong on the water, situations can become life threatening. Having a friend close by to help out could make a huge difference someday. If you are fishing in these more committing types of water and insist on paddling alone, it's only smart to take an open water or sea kayaking safety and rescue course.

The bottom line is, if you do decide to paddle alone, you need to be even more conservative than normal with all the decisions you make. You need to stay more alert and aware of your surroundings to minimize the chances of getting caught off guard and being left in a compromising position.

Kayak Fishing in Exposed Conditions

By Ken Whiting

When we talk about kayak fishing in exposed conditions, we're really talking about your exposure to wind and waves and your proximity to shore. As soon as you venture into water that isn't protected from wind and waves, and/or you travel further from shore than you can comfortably swim, you are entering a new world. You need to protect yourself by getting informed and developing practical rescue skills. It's a challenge well worth tackling! The skills and knowledge you'll gain from an open water kayaking course will not only protect you; it will provide a huge boost in confidence.

In this segment, we're going to talk about the major variables (which some would call hazards) that you might encounter in exposed water. Please understand that this is not designed to replace professional instruction, but to give people interested in venturing into exposed water a knowledge base, and to act as a refresher for those people who have already taken instruction. The reason I stress this is not because exposed water paddling needs to be a high risk activity. It doesn't! The problem is that if something goes wrong, an exposed water environment is one of the most unforgiving places to find yourself. For that reason, if you're going to venture onto the ocean or into a big body of water, it is highly recommended that you take an open water kayaking or sea kayaking rescue course.

Exposed Water Equipment Considerations

If you're going to travel and fish on open water, the equipment you decide to bring along will be less driven by preference and more driven by necessity—for safety's sake. Of course, every trip is different, so you'll need to decide which gear makes the most sense. The nice thing about kayaks is that there usually isn't any lack of storage space, so if you think there's even a small chance that you could use something, you might as well bring it.

SEAWORTHY KAYAKS

First of all, not every kayak is seaworthy for exposed water conditions. In particular, recreational sit-inside kayaks are inappropriate unless they have secure bulkheads and hatches with watertight compartments in both the bow and stern. These watertight compartments prevent the kayak from completely swamping (and potentially sinking) in the event of a capsize. They also make it much easier to perform any of the capsize recovery techniques, because your boat will be floating higher in the water. Any sit-inside kayak also needs to be used with a skirt in open water, to prevent the cockpit area from swamping .

For the kayak angler, a sit-on-top kayak is a much better choice because you don't have to worry about swamping. Furthermore, if you do capsize, it's much easier to hop back into the kayak.

Longer kayaks with rudders or skegs are also better for paddling in exposed conditions because they are faster and will travel straighter, with or without wind and waves to contend with.

SAFETY GEAR AND ACCESSORIES

In the first chapter, we took a look at the different pieces of safety gear that you need to consider. When fishing close to shore in sheltered areas, you may not need to bring anything beyond your PFD and a first aid kit. When paddling in exposed conditions, your safety gear needs grow considerably. Here's a quick list of the gear that you should bring, although it certainly doesn't represent an absolute list. It is very possible that the fishing conditions in your area warrant additional pieces of safety gear.

> **Water and Snack**

> **Spare Paddle**

> **First Aid Kit**

> **Navigation Tools**

> **Communication Devices**

> **Signaling Devices**

> **Emergency Kit**

> **Towline**

> **Bilge Pump (If you're paddling a sit-inside kayak)**

Communicating

When paddling in open water, paddle and whistle signals can come in really handy. Not only can your group get spread out very quickly, but wind will often make communicating by voice impossible. Of course, signals are only useful if everyone in your group knows how to interpret them, so it's worth going over them before heading out on the water. Here are some of the most basic and universal signals.

WHISTLE

- A single whistle blast is used to draw attention.
- Three short, sharp whistle blasts are used to indicate an emergency.

PADDLE

- A paddle held vertically into the air is used to communicate "go ahead."
- A paddle held horizontally into the air is used to communicate "stop."

BOAT SUPPORT

In many situations, it's only prudent (and practical) to have a powerboat for support when kayak fishing in open water. Not only will the powerboat let you move quickly from one fishing ground to the next, but it provides a quick means of escape in case the weather makes a quick turn for the worse. It can also provide valuable assistance for landing big fish.

Navigating

As you can imagine, getting lost on the water isn't any fun. In many cases, avoiding getting lost is as simple as following a shoreline, so you can just turn around and follow the same shoreline home. Throw a bunch of islands and some long crossings into the equation and you're opening the door to navigation woes. If you plan on entering a more complicated marine environment, you absolutely need to get trained in navigation techniques. This includes training in the use of a chart and compass, GPS, and tide and current tables, if they're relevant to your area. These are all topics that go beyond what we're able to cover in this book, although there are some good references available on the market. The best idea is to take a sea kayak navigation course.

A school of tarpon burst from the water in Boca Grande, Florida.

Towing

If you ever have to deal with an injured, seasick, or exhausted kayaker in open water, you might be in the position of having to tow them to shore. The most basic and most common means of towing someone is using a technique that sea kayakers call the "in-line tow." The in-line tow involves clipping a tow line onto the bow of the boat that you're going to tow. For long distances, you'll want to use a long towline (between 30 and 45 feet (9 to 14 meters) to avoid having the kayaks banging into each other. The towline should be attached to your body by a quick release belt that you can pop off at a moment's notice should the need arise.

Glossary of Terms

Assisted rescue – rescue technique performed with the aid of at least one other person in addition to the swimmer

Back band – a padded band of material that provides back support

Back face – the opposite side of the paddle blade from the power face, used for reverse strokes. Usually convex, with a spine along its center (also non-power face)

Bilge pump – a device for pumping water out of a boat

Body surfing – the position assumed when floating through whitewater; feet downstream, arms out to the side, and the whole body as close to the surface as possible

Bow – the front of a boat

Bowline – a cord attached to the front of the boat – useful for towing or tying the boat to a dock

Bulkhead – a waterproof wall that divides the interior of a kayak, creating flotation and storage areas

Bungee cords (also known as shock-cords) – elastic lines on the deck of a kayak, perfect for securing gear within easy reach (water bottles, sunscreen, ball cap, etc.); see also "Deck lines" and "Perimeter lines"

Capsize – when a boat overturns so that it goes from being right side up to upside-down

Cargo – the items transported in a boat

Chart (nautical) – marine map referencing water features, including depths, shorelines, scale, aids to navigation (like lights and buoys), and other features essential to marine navigation

Coaming – the lip around the cockpit that allows the attachment of a spray skirt

Cockpit – the sitting area in a kayak

Compass – a magnetic device that indicates magnetic north and the other corresponding points of direction over 360 degrees

Course – the compass direction of travel to a destination

Deck – the top of a kayak

Deck lines – a rope or shock-cord attached to a kayak's deck, used for securing items on deck or to make it easier to grab the boat; see also "Perimeter lines" and "Bungee cords"

Defensive swimming – passively swimming on your back, keeping as flat and shallow as possible with your feet downstream to fend off obstructions (also body surfing)

Downstream – the direction in which the water is flowing

Drain plug – a stopper, usually mounted in the stern, which can be removed to drain a kayak

Draw strokes – dynamic strokes designed to move the kayak laterally in the water

Drift fishing – a fishing technique that involves letting wind or current move the kayak over the area to be fished

Dry bag – a waterproof bag with a seal (usually a roll-top closing system) that keeps contents dry

Ebb tide – the outgoing tide and the resulting decrease in water depth; see also "Flood tide"

Eddy – the quiet water below an obstacle in current, where water flows back in the opposite direction to the main flow

Eddy line – the point along which the eddy current and the main current collide

Edging – to tilt your kayak to one side

Emergency bag – a dry bag that carries enough supplies to survive an unplanned night spent in the wilderness

Feather – the twist, offset, or difference in angles between the two blades of a kayak paddle

Ferry – the technique used to move laterally across the main current

Float plan – an outline of the route and schedule of a kayak trip

Flood tide – the incoming tide and the resulting increase in water depth; see also "Ebb tide"

Foot entrapment – when your foot gets stuck in riverbed debris

Foot pedals – foot supports that slide on a track to accommodate paddlers of different leg lengths; foot pedals also control the rudder, if a kayak has one

Foot wells – molded recesses in the deck of a kayak where you put your feet when sitting in a kayak

GPS (Global Positioning System) – a battery-powered electronic device that very accurately calculates positions and courses based on satellite information

Handles – the carrying toggles found at the bow and stern of a kayak

Hatch – the opening into a cargo compartment in a kayak

Hull – the bottom of a boat

Kayak – a watercraft propelled by a double-bladed paddle

Knot – a measurement of speed – one nautical mile per hour; see also "Nautical mile"

Life jacket – a flotation device worn like a vest

Mothership – a powerboat that can transport individual kayaks and anglers as a group to and from the fishing destination

Nautical mile – unit of distance used on the sea; approximately 1.87 kilometers or 1.15 "land" miles

Navigation – the art and skill of determining your position, and selecting a safe route to your intended destination

Paddle – a device used for propelling the boat by drawing its blades through the water; kayak paddles are double-bladed; canoe paddles have only one blade

Paddle leash – tether that attaches a paddle to a kayak

Perimeter lines – cords that run around the edges of the deck on a kayak, making the boat easier to grab; see also "Deck lines" and "Bungee cords"

PFD – Personal Flotation Device – see "Life jacket"

Portage – to carry a kayak or canoe overland

Power face – the concave side of a paddle blade that catches water during a forward stroke

Put-in – the location where a kayak trip begins; see also "Takeout"

Reentry – getting back into a kayak from the water

Rescue – a process whereby people at risk are returned to a situation of safety

Ripcord – the cord at the front of the spray skirt or spray deck that you pull to remove the skirt

Rip tide – strong current on a beach, created by waves; potentially very dangerous

Rocker – the curvature of a kayak's hull, as seen from the side

Rod holder – device for holding a fishing rod

Roof rack – system of two bars that mount to the roof of a vehicle for transporting kayaks and other loads

Rudder – a foot-controlled steering mechanism mounted at the back of a kayak

Scupper – a hole that goes through a boat, allowing water to drain off the deck back into the sea/lake/river

Self rescue – a rescue technique where the swimmer reenters the kayak without aid from a second party

Side-saddle – a sitting position that can be used for sit-on-tops with both legs hanging off one side of the kayak

SINK – acronym for a sit-inside kayak

Skeg – a blade or fin that drops into the water to help a kayak go straight

SOT – acronym for a sit-on-top kayak

Spray skirt (also called "spray deck") – nylon or neoprene skirt worn around the waist – attaches to the kayak coaming to keep water out of the boat

Stern – back of the boat

Strainer – a pile of logs or other debris that is stacked up by current over time, creating a major hazard for boaters

Takeout – the location where a paddling trip ends;

Tank well – molded recess in a kayak designed to carry a diver's oxygen tank

Thigh hook, or thigh brace – in some sit-inside kayaks, the curved flange that the leg braces against

Thigh straps – an after-market accessory that attaches to a sit-on-top to allow the kayak to be gripped by the paddler's legs

Tidal rip – a strong current created by changes in tide height

Tide and current tables (also collected in a "tide and current atlas") – the collected calculations for tide and current information (times, heights, speeds); organized based on the calendar year, so a recent version is required for accurate information

Trolling – a fishing technique that involves dragging a lure or bait behind a boat

VHF (Very High Frequency) – radio system commonly used in the marine environment; limited to a line-of-sight direct path between the transmitter and the receiver

Wind wave – waves formed by the effects of wind on the surface of water

IF YOU LIKED THIS BOOK, YOU'LL ALSO LIKE:

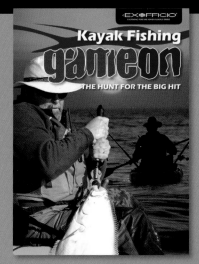

Kayak Fishing: GAME ON

An epic fishing movie that follows renowned big-game kayak angler, Jim Sammons, around North America on the kayak fishing adventure of a lifetime. Fights with tarpon in Florida, halibut in Alaska, 300 lb marlin in Baja, stripers in Chesapeake Bay, and muskie in Canada are just some of what you can expect to see in this exciting new film. The movie features action, adventure, valuable kayak fishing tips, and much more. Watch the trailer now at **www.kayakfishingmovie.com**

$29.95, 80 minutes

KAYAK FISHING
The Ultimate Guide

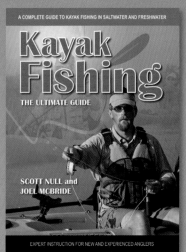

The ultimate DVD companion to this book! Whether you're a new kayak angler interested in developing a strong foundation of skills or a seasoned kayak angler who wants to get the most out of your time on the water, look no further—*The Ultimate Guide to Kayak Fishing* is the most comprehensive instructional DVD on the subject.

$19.95, 60 minutes

KAYAK FISHING TALES
Free WebTV Channel

The first and only online kayak fishing WebTV channel. A totally free online service, *Kayak Fishing Tales* features a new mini-episode every two weeks. You'll find kayak fishing tips and tricks, pro kayak angler profiles, destination features, and gear reviews.

Visit **www.kayakfishingtales.com** and subscribe now.

THE HELICONIA PRESS

1 888 582 2001
www.helipress.com